Data Modeling for the Business

A Handbook for Aligning the Business with IT using High-Level Data Models

first edition

Data Modeling for the Business

A Handbook for Aligning the Business with IT using High-Level Data Models

Steve Hoberman

Donna Burbank

Chris Bradley

Technics Publications
New Jersey

Published by:

Technics Publications, LLC

Post Office Box 161

Bradley Beach, NJ 07720 U.S.A.

www.technicspub.com/books.htm

Edited by Carol Lehn

Cover design by Mark Brye

Cartoons by Abby Denson, www.abbycomix.com

All of the data models in the text have been created using CA ERwin® Data Modeler. To learn more about this data modeling solution and to download a free trial, please visit www.ca.com/modeling.

This book is printed on recycled acid-free paper.

ISBN, print ed. 978-0-9771400-7-7

First Printing 2009

Printed in the United States of America

Library of Congress Control Number: 2008912011

CONTENTS

ACKNOWLEDGEMENTS

Thanks Carol, for the superb editing job, Mark, for the dynamite cover and Abby for the great cartoons. Thanks Mona, for your rich insights on the maintenance and marketing of the high-level data model.

Thanks Paul J. Arquette, AIA, for allowing us to use your architecture diagrams, Ted Burbank for your house plans, and CA for providing the CA ERwin® Data Modeler software for the sample models in the book.

Donna: I'd like to thank Eldora for giving me peace, quiet, and a 'room of one's own' in which to write this book. And special thanks to my Mom, who started me writing as a young child.

Steve: Thanks Jenn, for keeping my life sweet. Thanks Sadie and Jamie, for keeping me in the moment and reminding me to keep things simple.

INTRODUCTION

Has this ever happened to you? You have a credit card account with a particular financial institution. You've been using this card for years and regularly paying the balance from your checking account with that same institution. But each month, without fail, you get an advertisement in the mail to "Act now to sign up for a credit card!" Don't they know that you already have a credit card with them? Why are they wasting their money and your valuable time sending you annoying ads for something you already have? Don't they know better? Unfortunately, the answer is "No, they don't!", and at the root of the problem could very well be (you guessed it) an incorrect data model and processes put in place based on poor communication and documentation.

At the core of a data model is its usefulness in aligning the business and the data infrastructure that supports its applications. In this book, we'll go over some of the basics of what a data model is and why the core concepts stored in a high-level data model can have significant business impact on an organization. We'll explain the technical notation used for a data model and walk through some simple examples of building a high-level data model on your own. We'll also describe how data models relate to other key initiatives you may have heard of or may be implementing in your organization.

We'll discuss some best practices for implementing a high-level data model, along with some easy-to-use templates and guidelines for a step-by-step approach. Each step will be illustrated using many examples based on actual projects we have worked on. Names have been changed to protect the innocent, but the pain points and lessons have been preserved. One example spans an entire chapter and will allow you to practice building a high-level data model from beginning to end, and then compare your results to ours.

The best way to reinforce new information is to practice, practice, practice. Actually building a high-level data model following the ten step approach you'll read about is a great way to ensure you will retain the new skills you learn in this book.

As is the case in many disciplines, using the right tool for the right job is critical to the overall success of your high-level data model implementation. To help you in your tool selection process, we've dedicated a chapter to discussing what to look for in a high-level data modeling tool and a framework for choosing a data modeling tool, in general.

We'll conclude the book with a real-world case study that shows how an international energy company successfully used a high-level data model to streamline their information management practices.

Throughout this book, you'll find exercises that will help you practice new techniques and build data models that improve communication and increase alignment within your organization.

CHAPTER 1
What is a Data Model?

A data model is a visual representation of the people, places and things of interest to a business. It is used to facilitate communication between business people and technical people. A data model is composed of symbols that represent the concepts that must be communicated and agreed upon, and is therefore often referred to as a blueprint for data. Like a building architect, who creates a series of diagrams or blueprints from which a house can be constructed, a data modeler/architect creates diagrams from which a database may be built.

The blueprint analogy is often used because there are many parallels between blueprints, which many people are familiar with, and a data model, which few people outside of IT have seen. (Hopefully, this book will help to change that!). The most obvious parallel is that a blueprint translates a very complex and technical undertaking into a set of visual diagrams that a layperson can understand. This is the goal of a data model, as well—to take business concepts and the complex rules required to create a database and simplify them into an intuitive picture that both business people and technical engineers can understand. Just as a homeowner is involved in the design of their house before the technical design and building takes place, so, too, should business people be involved in the design of the data models from which the databases that run their organization are built.

Blueprints are created at several different levels of detail: from the high-level requirements, to the basic architectural layout, to the detailed wiring and plumbing designs. If you're getting ready to build a house, the architect normally starts by asking about your requirements—do you want a single story or multiple story building, a ranch or a cape? Do you want a front porch or a deck? How are you going to use this house? Will it be a vacation home or a full-time home for a large family? The architect uses these requirements to develop a series of diagrams for you to review. The first diagram is often a picture, or mock-up, of what the house might look like.

As a hypothetical example, let's say that I ask my architect for a small vacation home with a nice front porch. He might come back to me with this picture, showing an example of what the house could look like. See Figure 1.1.

Figure 1.1 – A Small, Wooden House with a Front Porch

Um...I was pleased that he was trying to keep my costs down, but I had something a little larger in mind. I should have been a little more precise about what I meant by 'small' and maybe he had a different definition of 'vacation'. What he showed me might work for an ice-fishing weekend, but it certainly wouldn't be appropriate for a week-long ski vacation with a dozen of my friends. And I had forgotten to mention that I wanted to retire there someday, so it really needed to function as a primary residence as well. I asked him to make it bigger and explained my requirements in more detail. I actually tried to draw it myself and created a rough sketch of what I had in mind, shown in Figure 1.2.

Figure 1.2 – A Small, Wooden House with a Front Porch

My picture was pretty simple, but from the combination of my verbal description and the picture that I drew, he had enough information to come up with a better design, shown in Figure 1.3.

Figure 1.3 – Architect's Sketch of House

This was just what I had in mind. Based on his experience in designing houses for other customers, my architect also made some suggestions about things that I hadn't thought of—like a heated garage for the winter and a second story with extra bedrooms for guests. I'm certainly glad we came to an understanding at this high-level before he started building! We saved a lot of expense and frustration that way. Once we agreed on the basic requirements for the house, the architect went a step further and drew a more detailed diagram to show the arrangement of the rooms, appliances, etc. There were several such diagrams, each with a particular focus to highlight an area of the house in detail. It would have been too confusing to see the entire house in a single diagram, so he broke up the diagram by floor: one for the main floor, one for the second floor, and another for the attic. He showed me the diagram for the main floor, a subset shown in Figure 1.4.

Figure 1.4 – Blueprint of a House (Subset Shown)

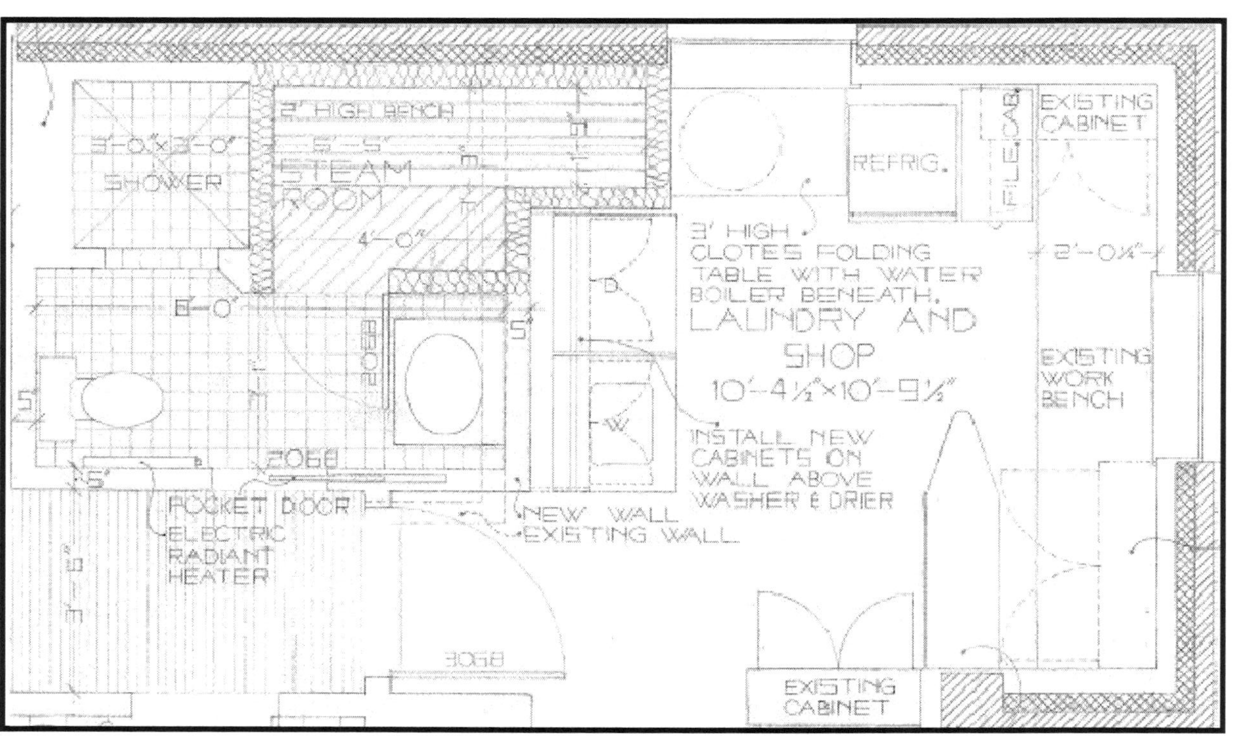

This gave me a much better sense of the details of the house. I wasn't initially sure what some of the symbols meant, but it didn't take me long to figure out that a slanted line meant that a door was opening in a certain direction and that double lines meant a window opening, etc. I got the basic idea, although I'm sure the builders would get much more from it than I did.

I was able to understand it well enough to change some of the mistakes that I saw, too. Once I saw everything laid out in the picture, I could get a better sense of how things fit together and the relationships between them. For example, I didn't want the master bedroom opening into the kitchen. I should have been clearer on these types of rules before, but (a) I wasn't able to articulate some things clearly enough to the architect and (b) I didn't realize there were mistakes until I saw them drawn out. Once I saw them in this picture, I was able to correct them easily. The picture was an excellent medium for communicating what the architect envisioned based on what I had told him and for me to identify and correct misunderstandings.

The architect then showed me the various wiring and plumbing diagrams, subset shown in Figure 1.5. These were much too technical for me to understand, but I'm glad somebody was taking care of this stuff. I definitely want the electricity to work, but don't bother me with the details.

Figure 1.5 – Physical Wiring Diagram (Subset Shown)

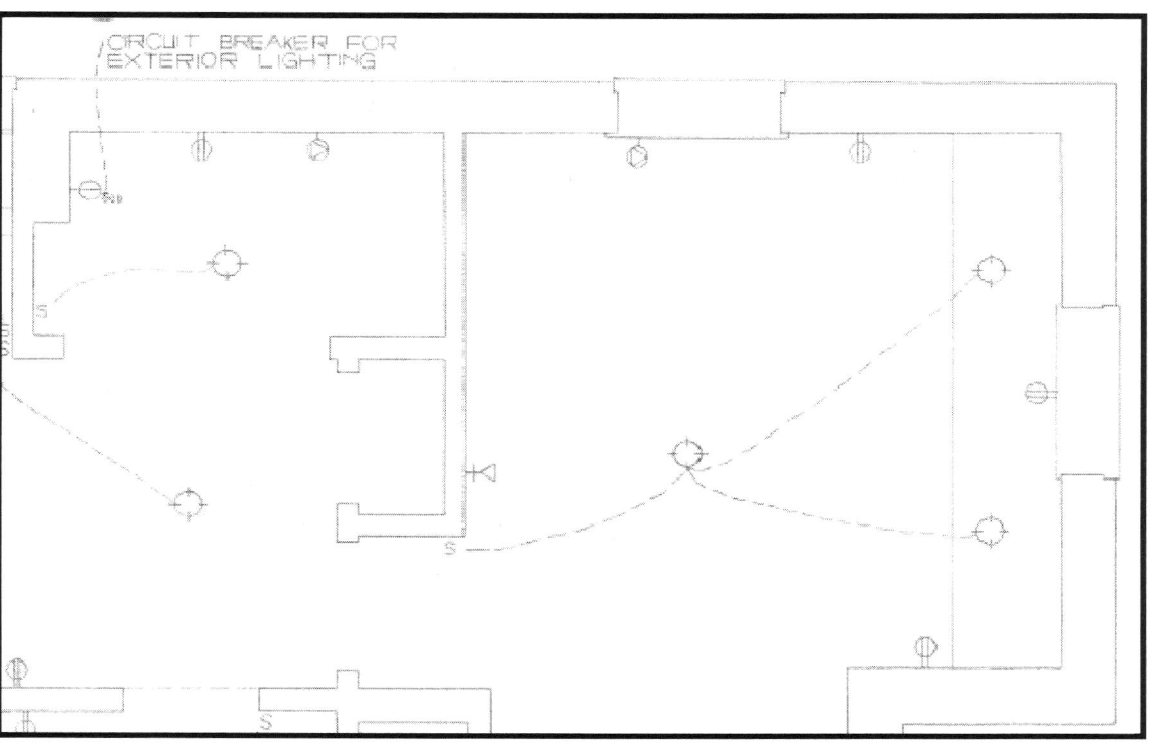

In this house example, we used several layers of diagrams: a very high-level picture to align on the scope of the project (Figure 1.1 and Figure 1.2), a high-level picture to ensure that we had the same vision of the house (Figure 1.3), then a more detailed layout of the architecture (Figure 1.4), and finally a detailed, technical design diagram of the physical infrastructure (Figure 1.5).

Each level of the blueprint has several components broken down by a particular function: a picture of the front of the house vs. the back; the layout of the first floor vs. the second, a physical wiring diagram vs. a plumbing diagram. Each level has a particular audience, owner and purpose. In the high-level diagrams, I was even able to do some of the design myself. As we got more detailed, however, I needed the expertise of an architect to fill out the structural specifications. Once we got to the physical layer, both the architect and I needed to bring in a technical contractor to build the diagrams. The same holds true for data models. We'll demonstrate some of the parallels in the rest of this chapter.

The chapters that follow will go into much greater detail on the different levels of data models and the high-level data model in particular, but to summarize, data modeling traditionally starts with a very high-level diagram to align on scope and common meaning, then a high-level picture to help gather business requirements and clarify understanding of basic concepts. The logical level follows, showing more detail while incorporating business logic and business rules. The physical level shows the technical details for implementation as a database or data structure.

This 'top-down' approach of starting with a very high-level design and moving successively into more detail is one way of looking at data design in an organization. Because we're often building on top of existing systems, it's more common to start from the 'bottom-up', similar to trying to visualize what the house is supposed to look like when only the physical wiring diagrams are shown. We'll go into more detail on various approaches to data design in Chapter 8 with top-down, bottom-up, and hybrid approaches. For now, suffice it to say that the real world is rarely as well-organized as we're describing here. We hope this book will help change that, at least for data management. World peace and an organized sock drawer come next.

Now, let's walk through an example of each of these levels with a corresponding example for both house design and data design. We started our house example by using a very high-level picture to describe the scope and basic requirements. I needed to clarify to my architect what I meant by 'house', what this house was going to be used for, and what was going to be included in the project. In a data model, we may use a picture containing a simple set of boxes that clarify the differences between, for example, a primary home and a vacation home. The house diagrams were created by the architect and me, a layperson. Similarly, in the data world, both a business person and a data architect would work together on the data model diagrams, with business people able to do much of the work themselves. See Figure 1.6 for an example of how a very high-level house diagram corresponds to a very high-level data diagram.

Figure 1.6 – Blueprint and Data Diagram at a Very High Level

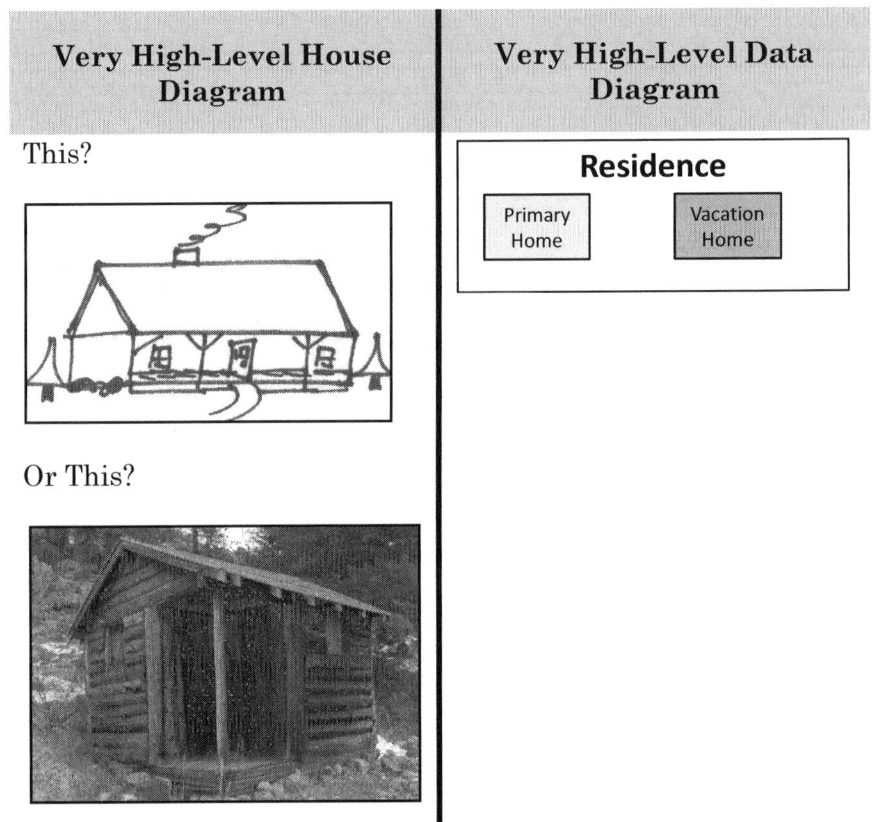

After we've reached consensus on what the scope of the project is, it's time to go deeper into the details of the design. For my house example, the architect drew a high-level picture to show what he had in mind for the house—that it would have a front porch, be big enough to sleep a large number of people, etc. For data, we use a high-level data model to clarify what information is important, how basic concepts are defined and how these concepts relate to each other.

In Figure 1.7, a set of boxes and lines clarifies what I mean by a 'house'. There is a textual description of a house and we also show how the concept of house relates to other concepts I had in mind. For example, a house isn't a 'house' to me unless it has a front porch; and it must have multiple bedrooms. We'll go into more detail regarding the exact notation for these models in Chapter 3, but for now, you should be able to understand what this model is trying to express.

Note again the roles involved in creating this level of diagram. I was collaborating closely with the architect, contributing content and examples. He might have guided me in this process, but I was heavily involved, so I felt a greater sense of ownership in having designed 'my' house.

Figure 1.7 – Blueprint and Data Diagram at a High Level

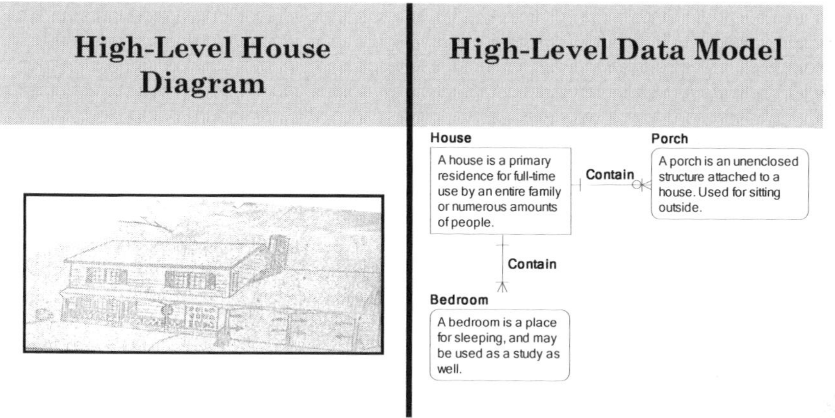

Once we've agreed on what a 'house' is, and how big of a project we have on our hands, we're ready to go into more detail. For the building architect, this means drawing out detailed floor plans to show the layout of the house, the size and use of the rooms, and how the rooms fit together. In data modeling, we have increasingly more detailed levels of the diagram to show the layout of the data, the size and type of the data, and how various objects relate to each other. See Figure 1.8.

Figure 1.8 – Blueprint and Data Diagram at the Logical Level

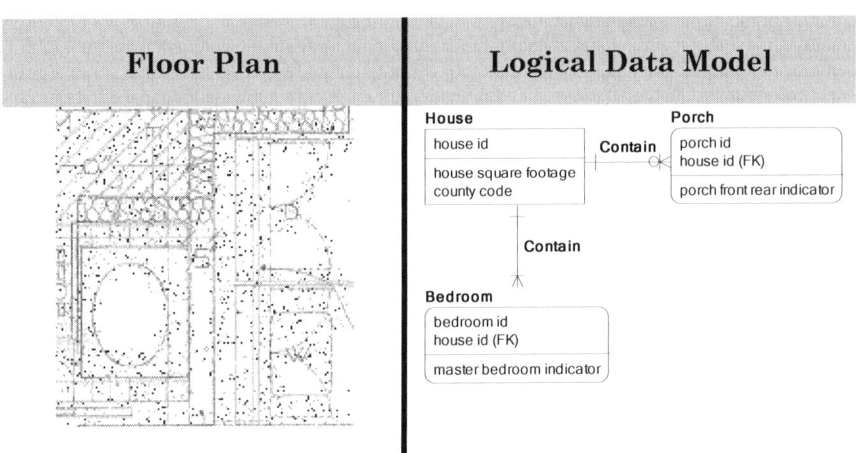

Note that for the house diagram, this level is created by the architect, with input and signoff from me. This also holds true in the data world. A logical data model is normally created by a data modeler/architect, but a business person needs to be heavily involved to make sure that the rules and definitions are represented correctly.

After the design of the house meets my needs and requirements, the architect passes the floor plans over to the contractor(s) who create the detailed wiring, plumbing diagrams, etc. Again, for data models, a similar paradigm holds true. While the physical diagram of a house explains how, for example, the wiring is laid out, the physical data model explains how the data is physically laid out and stored on a particular database platform. See Figure 1.9 for an example of a physical data model.

Figure 1.9 – Blueprint and Data Diagram at the Physical Level

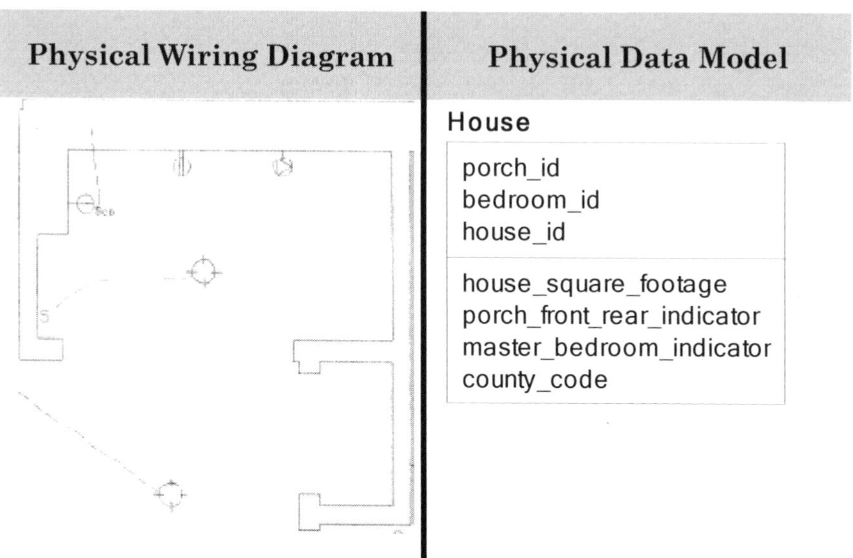

Just as this is normally handled by a contractor specializing in electrical work, for example, database design is often performed by a database administrator (DBA) who specializes in a particular database platform or architecture such as Oracle, Sybase, DB2, or XML. Remember, I really didn't want to see these diagrams—I just wanted to know that they were being built by someone with the right expertise. With data design, a business person should feel the same way. They don't have to be involved in the physical design of a database, but they should have confidence that the database is being designed and built by the appropriate staff.

From this analogy, you can see that a data model, like an architectural diagram for a house, is just a set of shapes and lines that help communicate meaning to both laypeople and technical engineers. We'll explain the notation in a step-by-step manner in Chapter 3, but you should already have a basic sense of what these models can convey just by looking at them.

You can also see from the house analogy that arriving at a common understanding is key to achieving a positive result. I needed to make sure that my architect shared my vision of what I'm looking for in a house. If he's designing a mansion, but I really wanted a small vacation home, the rest of the architectural details around wiring, plumbing, etc. are meaningless—I still wouldn't be happy with the end result. The same holds true in the world of data management and design—if the business people and stakeholders who are using the data are not involved in the design and are not happy with the key concepts in the data model, chances are the end results won't meet their needs and business performance will suffer as a result.

Key Points

- A data model is a visual representation of the people, places and things of interest to a business and is composed of a set of symbols that communicate concepts and their business rules
- Data models are similar to the architectural diagrams for a house in that they:
    - use a set of graphical images to convey technical information
    - consist of several levels, from a very-high level to describe scope, to a very detailed level describing technical details
    - show relationships between key concepts and objects
    - are used to facilitate communication

CHAPTER 2
Why Does a High-Level Data Model Matter?

A high-level data model conveys the core concepts and/or principles of an organization in a simple way, using concise descriptions. The advantage of developing the high-level model is that it facilitates arriving at common terminology and definitions of the concepts and principles.

> A high-level data model uses simple graphical images to describe core concepts and principles of an organization and what they mean.

Take a concept as simple as 'customer'. Everyone knows what a customer is, right? Or do they? The definition may change based on a person's perspective. To the billing department, a customer may be someone who owns a product or service sold by the company and to whom an invoice is sent. To a salesperson, a customer is someone who has not yet bought a product but to whom they hope to make a sale. And there are more things that we need to clarify... Does a customer have to be a person or can another company be considered a customer? Is someone who has purchased a product from us in the past, but does not have an active account, service agreement, or support contract still a customer? Is there a difference between an active and an inactive customer or an existing customer and a prospective customer? Let's take this last example and build a simple high-level data model to help explain these differences, shown in Figure 2.1.

Figure 2.1 – High-Level Data Model Showing Two Different Definitions of Customer

Customer	Customer
A person or organization who does not currently own any of our products and who is potentially interested in purchasing one or more of our products.	A person or organization that has purchased at least one of our products and has an active account.

"That's a high-level data model?" you may ask? "It's just a couple of boxes with text in them!" Yup! The key to a high-level data model is simplicity. An important goal of this model is to align on common terminology, business definitions and rules. The diagram can be as simple as a set of boxes with text in them, as in Figure 2.1. In future examples, we'll expand upon this simple model, adding more boxes and a few lines. But remember, a high-level data model should always be simple and clear enough that a non-technical, 'everyday' person can understand it.

"Isn't this too high-level to be useful?"

No, the purpose of the high-level data model is describing complex information in a simple way, using a concise description, not a vague one. $E=mc^2$ is a simple equation that communicates a complex idea to its intended audience using concise notation.

A high-level data model should focus on a particular area that's important to the audience or user, so that the content and scope is limited to the matter at hand.

Everything should be made as simple as possible, but not simpler. - Albert Einstein

In fact, a high-level data model doesn't even need to look like a traditional data model or be shown as a 'picture' at all. We could have placed the same information in a table or spreadsheet and come up with something like Figure 2.2.

Figure 2.2 – High-Level Data Model Shown in Table Format

Customer	A person or organization who does not currently own any of our products and who is potentially interested in purchasing one or more of our products.
Customer	A person or organization that has purchased at least one of our products and has an active account.

Both the diagram and the table format presentation highlight the issue of two different definitions of customer. A data modeling purist would correctly point out that you can't have two different definitions of customer on a 'valid' model.

While strict rules most definitely need to be followed on more detailed data models, the purpose of a high-level data model is communication and gaining consensus on core concepts so that the detailed diagrams created later are based on correct assumptions. It's okay to bend data modeling rules as long as the focus remains on aligning terminology, definitions and business rules. Looking back at the architecture example, if my architect started developing detailed floor plans and wiring diagrams for a three-story mansion when what I was looking for was a simple cabin, the end result wouldn't meet my needs no matter how good the design was.

High-level data models are the result of an iterative process. It is rare that the participants involved in creating the high-level data model will all agree on definitions when they are initially documented, but a first draft can be used to highlight differences of opinion so that discussions for achieving consensus can begin. Organizations and individuals may not even realize that there are different definitions until they are documented in this way. One technique for reaching consensus among the participants is to identify the various audiences, business areas, projects, applications, etc. that use each particular term. The meaning of a term can change based on its context, so it is critical to understand the context in which each term appears before consensus can be reached.

Let's go back to the credit card example in the introduction where you keep receiving offers for a new credit card even though you already have one. We'll perform our own mini data architecture project for the bank. Let's start by coming up with a list of all of the departments that access customer information. Our 'model' will be a simple list, shown in Figure 2.3.

Figure 2.3 – A Very High-Level Data Model Showing Stakeholders

Marketing
Consumer Credit
Banking

Identifying what data is used and by whom takes a lot of effort. It's much easier to focus on your own project or department, or at least it seems that way on the surface. But this siloed approach may lead to systems that don't work well together. By involving other groups, it's possible to leverage work that has already been done without reinventing the wheel.

Once the stakeholders are identified (people, groups or organizations that can affect or be affected by an action or policy), it's time to get them to talk to each other. In this case, after identifying and meeting with each of the organizations, the bank came to the conclusion that while the banking and consumer credit departments considered a 'customer' to be a person who had an existing account with the bank, marketing also used the term 'customer' to describe people who did not have an account with the bank.

These two definitions don't really conflict with each other; they represent different stages of the organization's relationship with the party. There are really two types of 'customers' – prospective customers, who have not yet purchased a good or service, and customers who have purchased a good or service and have an active account. We can change the model to reflect the two different meanings using the new terms 'Prospect' and 'Customer'.

If you think back to the blueprint analogy, the floor plan of the house not only helped me define what I was looking for, but it showed me how the rooms fit together—the relationships between them. High-level data models show how business concepts relate to each other. In fact, showing relationships, which represent business rules between concepts, is equally as important as creating good definitions. For the bank, we'll want to add a relationship that shows that a prospect is related to a customer in that once a prospect purchases a product, they become a customer. We use lines to show these relationships in a data model.

Figure 2.4 shows a simple high-level data model displaying both the definitions of the concepts and their relationships to each other.

Figure 2.4 – Data Model Clarifying the Definition of Customer

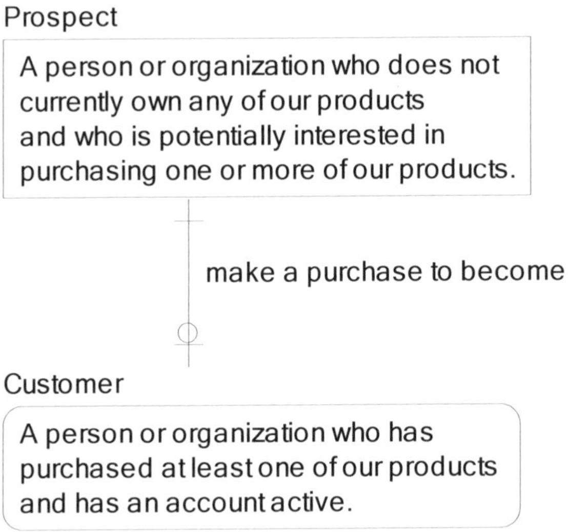

While this may be intellectually interesting, you may still be wondering what it has to with you getting ads from the bank for something you already have. As you just saw, when the bank developed their high-level data model, 'Customer' split into 'Prospect' and 'Customer', but this took place after their systems were already in operation. So when an employee in the marketing department for consumer credit logged into the bank's sales force web application and asked it to mail advertising about a credit card with a special interest rate to 'customers', the sales force web application then queried a database for a list of 'customers'. When building the database, the IT department was unaware that there were different meanings of the term customer, so both prospects and customers were included and were indistinguishable from each other. The sales force web application extracted a list from the customer database containing both customers and prospects. So you, the innocent customer, received a mailing that really should have gone to prospects.

Integration

Now that you understand why you're receiving erroneous marketing ads and have contacted the bank offering your data architecture services to solve their problem at a discounted rate, you're feeling confident and happy. But the next day you go to your mailbox and shake your head in frustration. Since you have both a checking account and a credit card account with this bank, you'd assume that you would get all of your records on a single statement. But no! You receive a bank statement addressed to 'Jane W. Doe', and a separate credit card statement addressed to 'Jane Doe'. How can they not know you're the same person?

Let's go back to the list of business areas we put together in the last section. We used that list to contact each organization to understand how each defined customer. From that we determined that the marketing department's information should really be stored and/or accessed differently from that of consumer credit and banking. Creating this list is a fairly simple task for our small example, but for a large organization, it can be a daunting one. It may take months or even years to get a true assessment of what information a company has and which departments or applications are using it. If it is difficult to merely document what information exists, imagine how much harder it is to make sure the information is accurate, consistent, and stored the same way.

In many companies, each department stores its information in its own database, cut off from other groups in the organization. Common terminology, definitions, and rules across departments and projects can break through these silos, enabling the organization to operate as a single, powerful unit. You may have heard the terms Master Data Management, Customer Data Integration, Enterprise Architecture, and Data Warehousing. All of these are initiatives that attack the lack of integration from different angles, and all of them require an accurate data model to be successful. See Chapter 7 for more information on how a high-level data model can aid these initiatives.

For our simple example, let's take the list of departments and map which departments use which customer information, shown in Figure 2.5.

Figure 2.5 – Mapping Business Areas to Common Terms

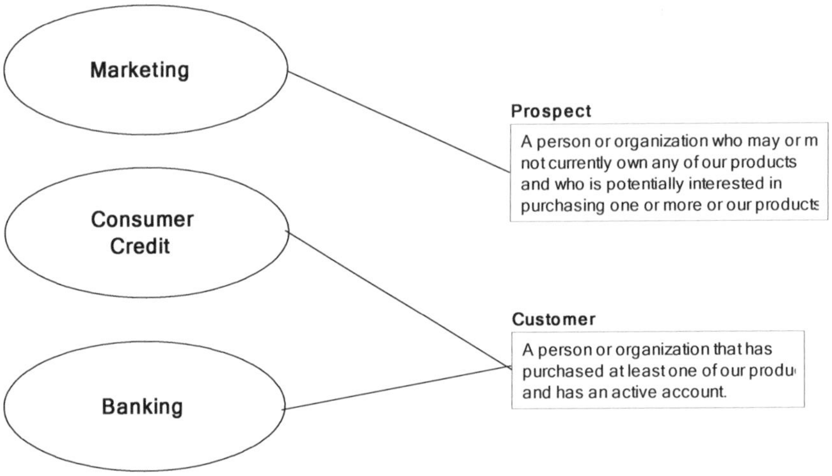

Marketing

Consumer Credit

Banking

Prospect

A person or organization who may or m not currently own any of our products and who is potentially interested in purchasing one or more or our products

Customer

A person or organization that has purchased at least one of our produ and has an active account.

This is the first step towards developing a single statement with both your banking and credit card information. Now, at least, the departments can see that they are using the same data. They have an opportunity to share it and take advantage of new data created by the other department. Since the Banking and Consumer Credit departments know that they are both using the same information, they can just combine their data in a single place to get you an integrated statement, right? Ah, if only it were that simple!

You'll recall from our earlier discussion that the purpose of a data model is to not only document the definitions for and context around information, but also to document the actual physical structure of the databases in which the information is stored. The same information can be stored with many different names, formats, and software platforms, so after we have documented how the data *should* be, we still need to map

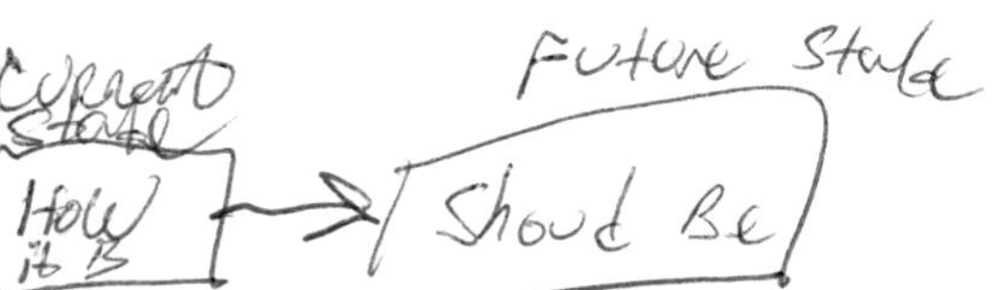

how it is *today*. This leads us to a discussion of the importance of standards and reuse.

Standards and Reuse

Now that we know that two departments are using the same definition of customer, can we ensure that the information they use is truly the same? In Figure 2.6, we see the different types of information about customers that are stored by each department. A good high-level data model should be basically understandable even if you don't recognize the notation used. Just like the floor plan of your house, it should provide a clear overview that's easily understood. So for now, ignore the notation and just look at the information that we're tracking about customers in the two business areas: Consumer Credit and Banking.

Figure 2.6 – Differences in the Customer Information Stored in Different Departments

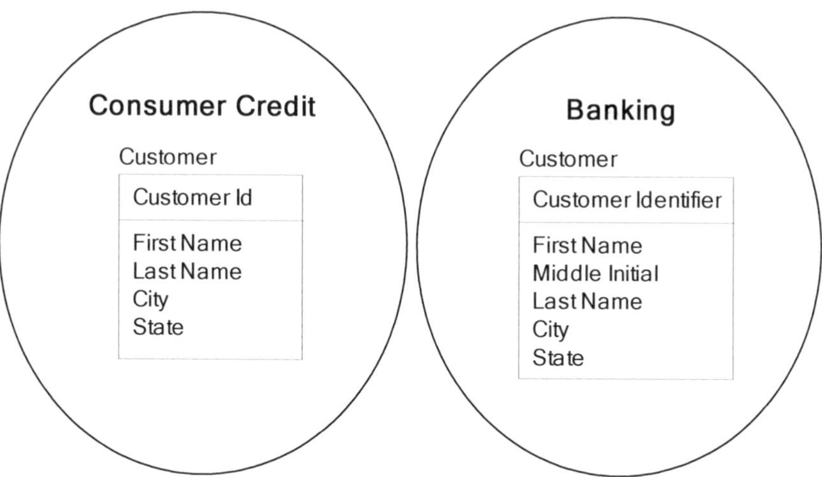

You'll see that the information is basically the same—the customer's name, location, and an identifier for the customer. But you'll also notice there are subtle differences. Consumer Credit uses the term 'Customer Id' while Banking spells it out as 'Customer Identifier'. In our first example, we found that differences in the meaning of the word customer could have negative effects. In this example, the meaning of the customer identifier field is exactly the same, but different terms are used to describe it. A human could easily determine that 'Customer Id' and 'Customer Identifier' are the same thing (although we should always verify this to be sure), but a computer cannot. Thus, to truly integrate these systems, we would have to use common naming standards to make sure that we can match information correctly. Again, this is an easy enough task in the simple example shown in Figure 2.6, but can take months or years in a large organization with thousands or even millions of different pieces of information to keep track of.

You'll also see that Banking stores a middle initial for a name, but Consumer Credit does not. This might cause a problem when matching or reporting data. To truly integrate these two departments, we need to identify:

- Common meaning of terms
- Which groups, applications or organizations are using the information and for what purpose
- Standard naming conventions for terms with the same meaning
- Standard design structures for the information

Once we've tackled all of the above, the truly difficult part begins. To this point, we've only aligned on the common meaning, purpose, and design of our information. We haven't begun to address the actual data content or the way it is physically stored. That challenge, which is beyond the scope of this book, is akin to changing the wings on an airplane as it's flying across the Atlantic. The database systems that need to be changed are in use by the mission-critical applications that are running your business; and as we've seen, they are used by many areas across the organization. Before any data is changed, the effect that this change would have on existing systems must be carefully assessed.

So you might be waiting a while before you are able to get your single bank and credit card statement, but at least we were successful in stopping the marketing department from continuing to send you unwanted mail!

Data Modeling for All

As you've seen, arriving at common goals, scope, and context and creating a common understanding of core concepts of the business across functional areas is critical to a successful data management program. They are the reasons we build a high-level data model. It is important that the IT systems that manage the data in your organization are based upon *your* understanding of information, and the business rules that define *your* organization. While business people do not need to be involved in the physical design of database systems, they do need to be involved in the high-level data models that define these database systems. It is the goal of this book to make the process of building a high-level data model an achievable goal for the average business user.

I (Donna) recently enrolled in a mountaineering and avalanche safety course, in which the instructor stressed the importance of a *common mental model* to ensure the safety of the group. A high percentage of deadly accidents that occur in the backcountry are the result of a different mental image of what a "day of skiing" entails. One member of the group wanted to descend a steep vertical glacier, while the other members wanted an easy day of flat touring. Members ended up splitting up and doing their own thing, unable to help each other if disaster struck. I tried to tell my instructor that this siloed-approach is common in data architecture as well, and suggested building a high-level data model for the group. I ended up skiing alone that day but, nonetheless, the following quote stuck in my mind:

"Teams operate as knowledge systems, and the building of shared mental models and the collective consciousness of the team mind creates a highly efficient context within which ... judgment and decisions can occur."

- Laura Adams, in "Avalanche Judgment and Decision Making"

Now You Try It! Let's Build a High-Level Data Model

Building a shared mental model is important in many aspects of life—from building a house, to surviving a mountaineering expedition, to implementing a database system. How many mistakes could have been avoided had we taken the time to stop and make sure everyone on the team had the same goals and objectives and that the meaning of each other's words were well-understood?

Let's use a family vacation as an example. Many vacations have been ruined by the fact that each member of the family had a different idea of what vacation meant to them. Mom wanted a vacation where she could relax and read a book. Dad wanted to drive across the U.S. to visit the 11 states that he hadn't seen yet. Jane wanted to get outside and hike because she had been inside studying for finals for weeks. And Bobby wanted to stay home and spend time with his friends. When Dad packed everyone into the car for a 'fun' vacation, the rest of the 'team' was miserable.

Perhaps they could have created a high level data model to define what the concept of vacation meant to each of them, as in Figure 2.7.

Figure 2.7 – Different Definitions of 'Vacation'

Person	Concept	Definition
Dad	Vacation	An opportunity to take the time to achieve new goals.
Mom	Vacation	Time to relax and read a book.
Jane	Vacation	A chance to get outside and exercise.
Bobby	Vacation	Time to be with friends.

Now you try it. Ask each member of your family, or a group of your friends, what they mean by vacation. Write down the responses in a table similar to the one above. Now, for extra credit, try to get everyone to agree on a *single* definition of vacation.

Key Points

- A high-level data model defines the core definitions and business rules on which the applications and database systems that run an organization are built
- Not having a common understanding of terms, such as 'customer', can have tangible, negative business consequences
- Arriving at common definitions in a high-level data model is key to integration efforts
- A high-level data model doesn't have to be complicated—it can be as simple as a text-based list of business terms and their definitions
- Business people can and should have a hand in creating the high-level data models that define their business
- A main goal of a high-level data model is communication between the business and IT

CHAPTER 3
A More Detailed Look at the High-Level Data Model

In the previous chapter, we covered why a high-level data model is important and gave you a very rough sense of what a data model is. We've been fairly loose with our terms and definitions, however, just to get the basic concepts around data models across before delving into more technical aspects. In fact, that's a strategy we'll stress throughout the book—while precision of language is important, it's also important to cater your language and approach to your audience to ensure information is communicated effectively.

It's the yin and yang of high-level data modeling—being precise where it's important for the ultimate goal of the project, but being flexible enough to bend the rules when it helps the audience understand the meaning of the model (Figure 3.1). Again, the ultimate goal of any data model is ***communication***.

Figure 3.1 – The Yin and Yang of Data Modeling: Balancing Precision with Flexibility

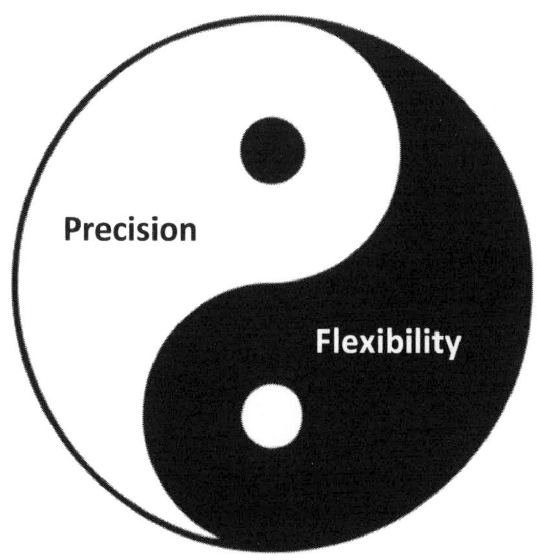

In this chapter, we'll explore the different levels of data models, from very high-level models aimed at the business audience, to detailed technical models aimed at developers who are implementing physical database systems. While the focus of this book is the high-level data model, we want you to understand how the detailed models relate to high-level data models.

The more detailed models contain all of the data elements specified in the requirements in a very precise format, facilitating moving from high level to details without loss of information, thereby allowing the database administrators and developers to build systems that match the requirements. These more detailed models are the 'yang' of the data world—they are actionable, precise, and powerful in that they support creation of the systems that run a company. Because of this, and also because it is IT who often creates these models rather than the business people, they are seen as more important than high-level data models, which focus on the 'softer' side such as communication and collaboration.

When building a high-level data model, it is important to remember the 'yin' of data modeling—to be flexible and listen to others. It takes both the yin and the yang, to build a successful high-level data model. While precision and rules should be followed, it's important to be flexible and yield the rules when it helps to enable communication and the ability to capture the requirements of the business.

This book will give you some practical tips on when strict notation is needed and when the rules can be loosened to get the point across to various audiences. If your goal is to get several groups to agree on a common definition of customer, it's the *definition* that's important, not the notation used to help discover the definition. If it takes placing sticky notes on a wall, or having each group make t-shirts with their particular definition on it, or having a plane fly overhead spelling out the definitions with its tail smoke to reach consensus, so be it. But sometimes, notational artifacts can help explain subtle differences in meaning which will affect implementation later on. We'll walk through some of these notations and explain why they are important.

Now let's define the levels of data models used in an organization more rigorously. There are traditionally four levels of data models. Each applies to a different audience and has a unique purpose. Figure 3.2 shows how these levels relate to each other and the sections that follow go into more detail on each.

Figure 3.2 – Levels of Data Models

- One Pager
- Agreement on 'Big Picture' Terms and Definitions
- Audience = Business Users

- One Pager (maybe 2)
- Defines core terms/definitions + business logic
- Audience = Business Users and Analysts

- > 1 Page
- Defines relational or dimensional structures independent of technology
- Audience = Business Analysts & Architects

- > 1 Page
- Defines relational or dimensional structures tuned for technology
- Audience = Architects, DBAs, Developers

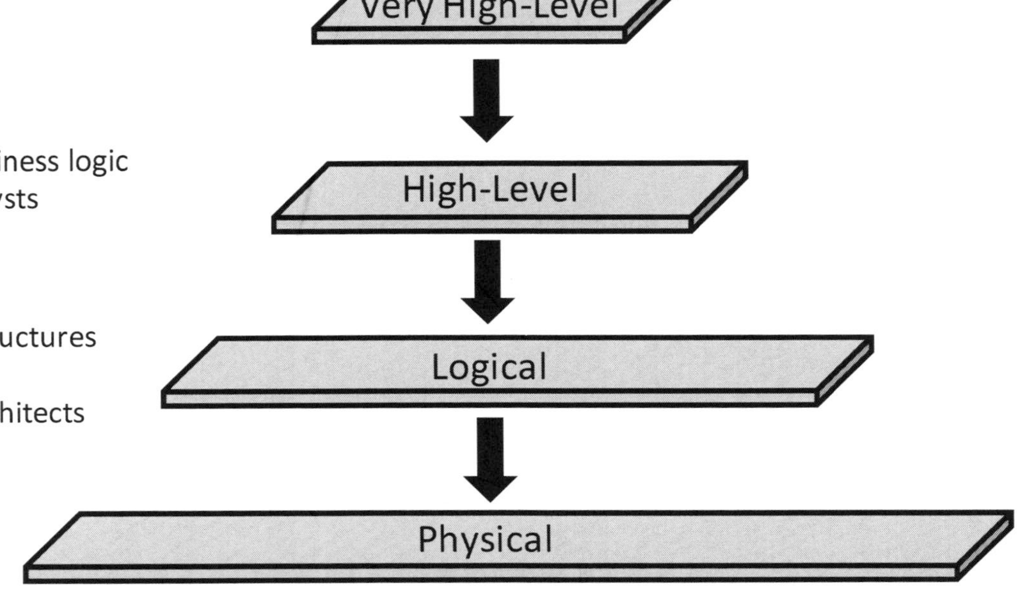

Very High-level Data Model (VHDM)

The purpose of a very high-level data model (VHDM) is to provide an organized structure from which the high-level data model and other model levels can be developed. Objects on this model represent the basic *subjects* of the modeling effort, which may be: business areas, subject areas, applications, or stakeholder viewpoints. The relationships between the subjects may also be represented.

In terms of rules and guidelines, this model level is the most flexible. Formal modeling notation is less important than in other levels. The subjects shown on this model are often represented by boxes or circles, pictures, or even plain text. The key is to graphically create an organized structure to which more detailed data concepts in the lower model levels can be mapped.

The number of concepts represented on this model should be small. Ideally, it should fit on one page and be easy to read. While this model is critical for large applications and enterprise architecture initiatives, for smaller modeling efforts that may deal with only a single stakeholder, this model level could be considered optional.

Let's start by defining the objects that are included in a VHDM:

Subject: Each subject represents an area of scope for the model—business areas, subject areas, applications, or stakeholder viewpoints. A subject can be represented by any graphical or textual image. It is commonly displayed as a box or an oval on a graphical diagram.

Relationship: A relationship defines the hierarchy of subjects on the VHDM and is represented by a solid line. Relationships are optional, but are shown on the majority of the VHDMs we've seen used in practice. Whether to use relationship lines or not depends on your purpose. If your main goal is to group information into functional areas, they may not be needed. If you need to represent how the various subjects fit together, relationship lines are required.

We've mentioned that the VHDM is the most visually flexible of the model levels. Subjects can be represented in many ways. Below are some examples of VHDMs.

In the VHDM in Figure 3.3, information is grouped by high-level subject, such as customer, product, etc.

Figure 3.3 – Example of a VHDM Representing High-Level Subjects

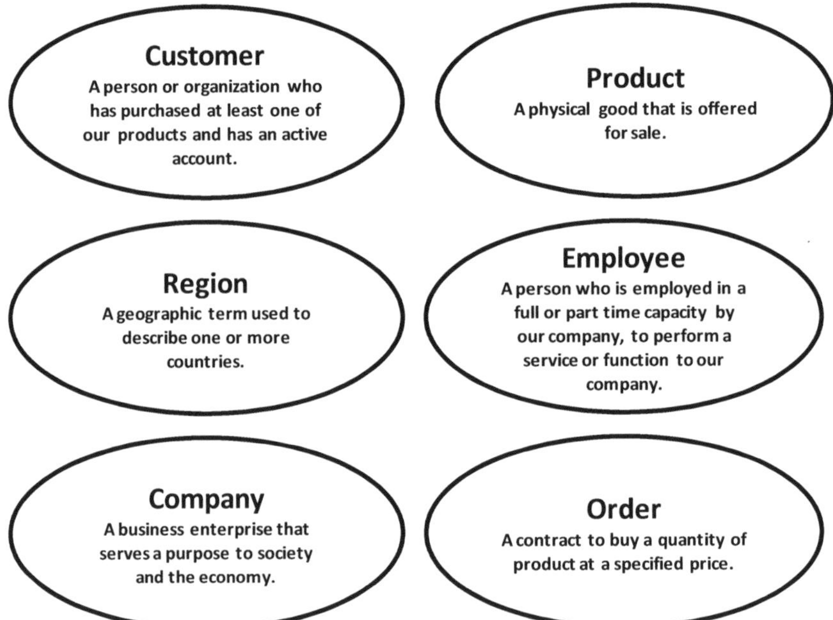

In Figure 3.4, the VHDM represents business areas across the organization.

Figure 3.4 – Example of a VHDM Representing Business Areas

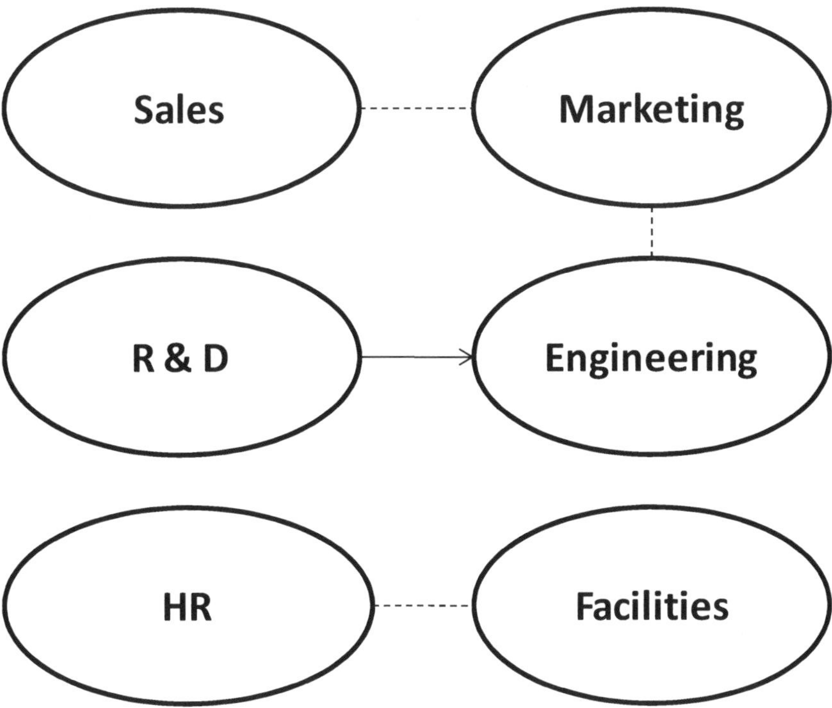

Each business area is represented by an oval, but any shape or graphical image could be used, as shown in Figure 3.5. Simple lines can be used to indicate organizational hierarchy. For example, Sales has a 'dotted line' to Marketing. These business areas would be used to group information. Sales, for example, might contain product, order, and customer information.

Figure 3.5 – Using Graphics for a VHDM

High-Level Data Model (HDM)

A High-Level Data Model (HDM) is used to communicate core data concepts, rules, and definitions to a business user as part of an overall application development or enterprise initiative. The number of objects should be very small and focused on key concepts. Try to limit this model to one page, although for extremely large organizations or complex projects, the model might span two or more pages.

The HDM is normally shown as a simple box-and-line diagram with names and definitions associated with the boxes. The HDM conveys the scope and definitions of the modeling effort, not what data will be captured—that will come later. An example of a HDM is shown in Figure 3.6.

Figure 3.6 – Example of a HDM

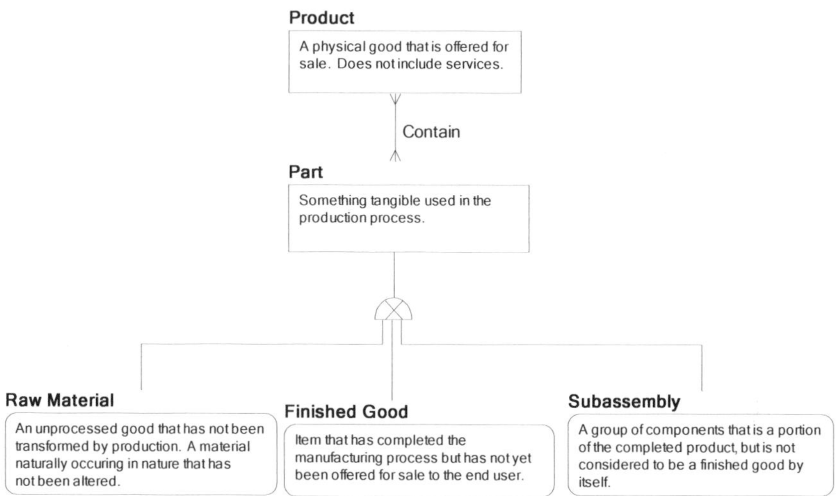

In this example, we're drilling down into the 'Product' subject in the VHDM to see more detail around product information. Even without understanding the notation, you can get the sense that this diagram is showing that a product consists of one or more parts, which could be a raw material, a finished product, or a subassembly.

This is a very simple example, but you can see that by drilling into the Product subject from the VHDM, you get a more refined view of the information related to products. Figure 3.7 shows how the objects on the VHDM and HDM map to each other.

Figure 3.7 – Product Subject on the VHDM Maps to the Product HDM

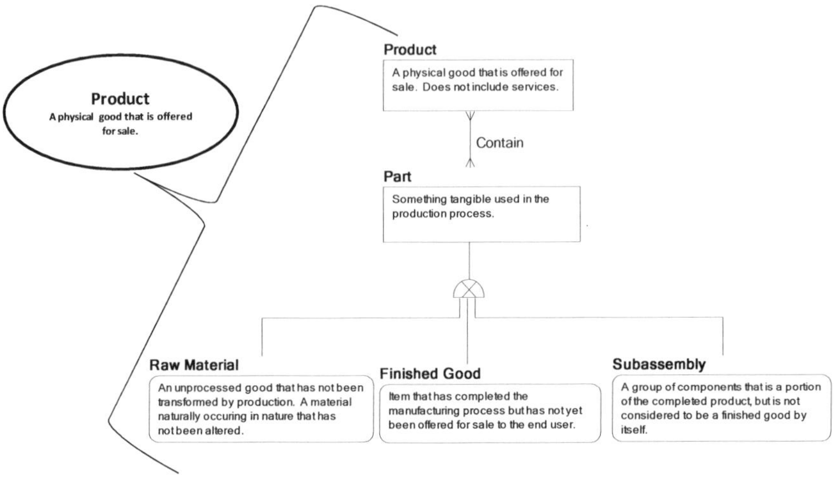

Product
A physical good that is offered for sale.
Product
A physical good that is offered for sale. Does not include services.
Contain
Part
Something tangible used in the production process.
Raw Material
An unprocessed good that has not been transformed by production. A material naturally occuring in nature that has not been altered.
Finished Good
Item that has completed the manufacturing process but has not yet been offered for sale to the end user.
Subassembly
A group of components that is a portion of the completed product, but is not considered to be a finished good by itself.

Focusing on a different business area in the VHDM such as 'Sales', for example, would give us something like Figure 3.8.

Figure 3.8 – Sales HDM

Customer
A person or organization who has purchased at least one of our products and has an active account.
Place
Order
A contract to buy a quantity of product at a specific price.
Appear on
Product
A physical good that is offered for sale. Does not include services.

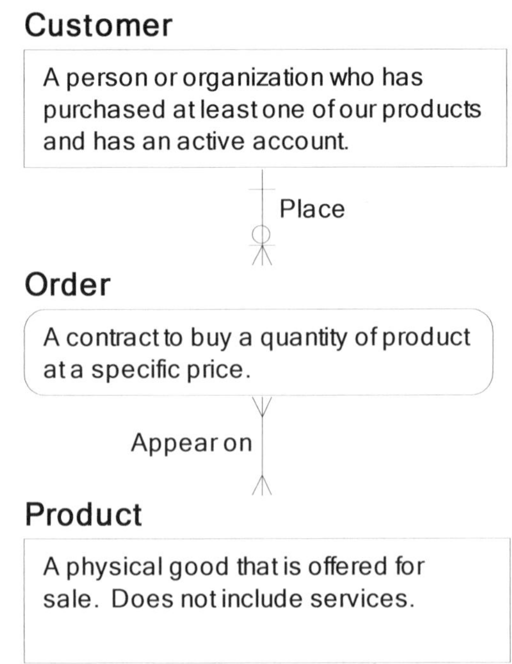

In building a HDM, it's important to choose both the ***focus*** and ***purpose*** of the model. It's nearly impossible to model the entire enterprise at once—that would take years. A better approach is to start with small, manageable 'chunks' of the business and show incremental value at each step before moving on to the next. To that end, each model should have a clear focus. For example, you may choose to focus on a particular area of the business or a business process such as Credit Applications. Or you may choose to start with a particular application, such as an SAP module that needs to be integrated with a legacy system. Whatever the focus, it should be clearly defined and documented before the model is built.

Equally important is to choose the purpose of the HDM, which will determine what type of model to build. A HDM may be used to support operational (transactional) systems or reporting systems. The modeling techniques are different for each: a relational data model is used for operational systems and a dimensional data model is used for reporting.

Relational (Operational): Supports one or more applications that run the business. It captures the concepts and business rules that are needed to support applications. For example, a HDM for an online store for a retail organization would need to capture the business concepts around product, orders, customers, credit, etc. It would also need to capture the rules supporting the application, such as the fact that a customer can only have a single line of credit, or that an order may contain multiple products that are shipped together. An easy way to think of this is to consider that the ***relational*** model shows how these business concepts ***relate*** to each other.

Dimensional (Reporting): Shows how concepts are used for reporting, usually in association with data warehousing and business intelligence applications. There's a set of 'facts' that represents the numbers resulting from doing business—for example the number of units of a product sold last week, the amount received from the sale of the units, the cost of producing those units, etc. The facts are related to 'dimensions'—categories of information that can be used to look up characteristics about what the facts refer to. For example, product is a dimension that might provide the name of the product that was sold, perhaps its size and weight, the barcode associated with it, its wholesale price, where it is produced, etc. A dimensional model enables slicing and dicing of information in many ways so that the business can analyze the data.

Table 3.1 shows the different HDM Focus areas and Functions.

Table 3.1 – Identifying Focus and Function

Focus of model	Function of model: Operational (Relational)	Function of model: Reporting (Dimensional)
Business Area, Functional Area, Subject Area, Business Process, or Enterprise View	Choose when capturing how the business works and there is a need to understand a business area, design an enterprise data model, or start a new development effort.	Choose when capturing how the business does reporting and there is a need to visually capture the information the business uses to calculate its metrics. That is, view metrics at different levels of granularity, such as Month and Year.
Application or Program	Choose when capturing how the application works and there is a need to understand an existing or proposed application, or start a new development effort.	Choose when capturing how the business is monitored through a particular application. The application allows users to view metrics at different levels of granularity, such as Month and Year.

We'll talk more about how to choose which type of model to use for your project in Chapter 8.

Logical Data Model

A logical data model (LDM) is a graphical representation of the people, places and things of interest to the organization (entities), the core business rules governing them, the relationships between them and all of the characteristics about each of them that are needed to run the applications of the business. The LDM shows more details than the HDM, and is independent of any physical implementation.

A sample logical data model based on our Sales HDM is shown in Figure 3.9.

Figure 3.9 – Sales Logical Data Model

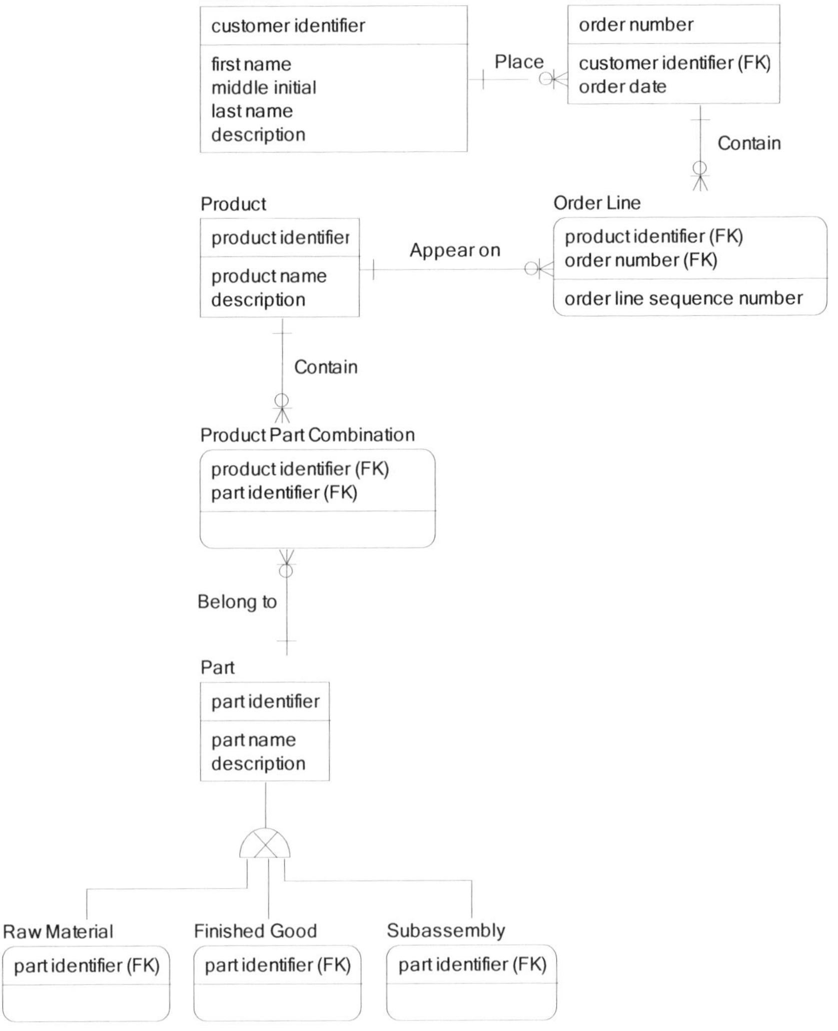

Physical Data Model

A physical data model (PDM) is a graphical representation of the physical structure of an actual database or data structure. The physical data model may contain components of the logical data model that have been modified or combined to optimize database and application performance. Logical entities can become physical tables and business rules can become database constraints. Other database techniques for improving performance such as indexing and partitioning may also be represented in the physical data model. A physical data model is usually designed and optimized specifically for the technology in which it will be implemented.

Some common types of implementation technologies include:

- **Relational database**. Relational databases store large amounts of data in tables and are probably the most common target structures for physical data models. Some of the common relational database platforms are Oracle and Microsoft SQL Server. In fact, relational databases are so common that we usually neglect to add the 'relational' and just say 'database'. Each vendor's implementation of relational database management system is slightly different, so it's helpful to have separate physical data models for each platform to optimize performance.
- **XML Schema**. Extensible Markup Language (XML) is the technology that underlies most of the web applications that you use. A detailed explanation of XML is beyond the scope of this book, but an easy way to look at the difference between XML and a relational database is while a relational database is designed to store large quantities of data, XML is designed to transport, share, and display information via the internet.
- **Legacy Data**. The term 'legacy' has become an all encompassing term for older technologies that were around before relational databases. It includes other forms of data storage such as flat files or VSAM, for example, which don't have a relational structure. Many of the mainframe applications that still power organizations today run on legacy storage structures. Note: Be careful. One person's 'legacy' is another person's 'new technology'. We definitely started to feel

> old when 20-year old application developers referred to applications built for relational databases as 'legacy' applications.

A sample physical data model for a relational database, based on the Sales LDM, is shown in Figure 3.10. This book isn't addressing PDMs in detail, so just remember the key point that a PDM is optimized for database performance and shows the technical implementation details for a particular database platform or technology.

Figure 3.10 – Sales Physical Data Model

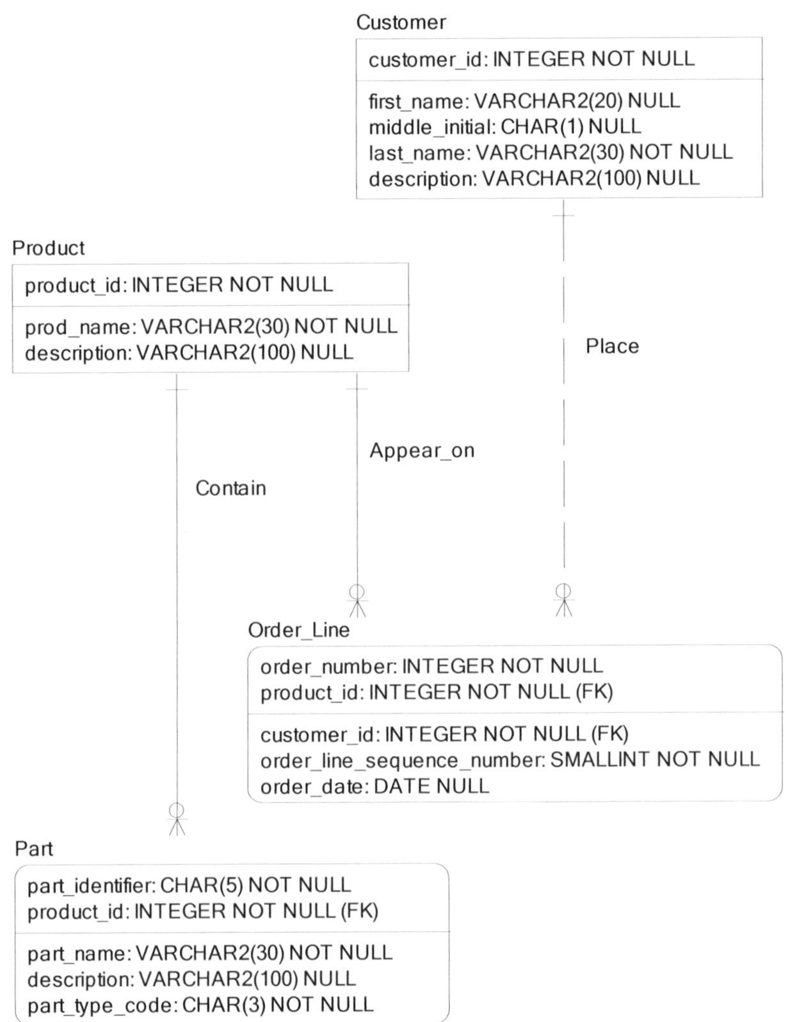

How the Four Levels of Detail Fit Together

The table in Table 3.2 shows the basic object mapping between the four layers:

Table 3.2 – Object mapping between model layers

VHDM Object	HDM Object	LDM Object	PDM Object
Subject	Concept	Entity	Table
Relationship	Relationship	Relationship	Constraints

This concept of **linking** or **mapping** between different design levels is important to high-level data modeling. We stress the importance of integration and information sharing throughout the book. The ability to link your high-level data models to the lower-level data models that control your business rules and ultimately the database systems that run the organization is key to this integration.

For example, we've seen how a very high-level concept such as Product eventually translates into one or more database tables at the physical level. The technical terms for this translation are **forward-engineering** and **reverse-engineering**. Think of forward-engineering as going from a higher level to a lower level and reverse-engineering as the reverse of that. So if we start at the 'top' and create a logical data model from a high-level data model, we'd call it forward engineering. If we create an inventory of the physical database tables and generalize them 'up' into a logical data model and eventually a high-level data model to link them to a single business concept, we'd call that reverse engineering.

Why is this linking and forward/reverse engineering important? In most organizations, a single definition of

Customer can be implemented in hundreds of database tables on a variety of database platforms. For example, a table might be called 'cust' in the Sales database in Oracle and 'customer' in the Trading database in Sybase, and so on. If we change the business definition of customer from, for instance, individuals who must have an active account to include individuals who may have had an account in the past, we need to change the information that is stored in the physical database tables. We'd need to perform an impact analysis to see which tables and applications were affected by the change. The linkage between the model levels would allow you to start at the HDM, trace the concept to all of the LDMs it appears in and then trace it further to all of the PDMs representing the actual tables that have been implemented.

The chart shown in Table 3.3 summarizes some specific differences between the various levels of models. In general, it may be helpful to keep the following in mind:

- VHDM is for ***Scope***
- HDM is for ***Need*** (i.e. what does the business need?)
- LDM is for ***Business Solution***

Table 3.3 – Comparing the Model Levels

	VHDM	HDM	LDM
Model Content	Defines the scope, audience, context for information	Defines key business concepts and their definitions	Represents the data needed, business rules and data relationships at a detailed level
Model Purpose	Communication and agreement on scope and context	Communication and agreement on definitions and business logic	Provides enough detail for subsequent first cut physical design
Relation-ships	Relationships optional. If shown, represent hierarchy.	Many-to-Many relationships OK	Many-to-Many relationships resolved into new entities
Naming Conventions	Subject names should represent subjects or functional areas	Concept names should use business terminology	Entity names should describe what data the entity contains
Diagram Size	One page	*Usually* one page	Often larger than one page
Participants in Developing Data Model	Business-driven	Cross-functional and more senior people involved in HDM process with fewer IT.	Multiple smaller groups of specialists and IT folks involved in LDM process.
Notation Used	Informal notation	Some formatted constructs needed, yet simplicity chosen over precision	Formal notation required
Number of Objects	< 20 objects	< 100 objects	> 100 objects

Components of a HDM

Now let's take a look at the parts of a HDM and discuss some of the guidelines and techniques for building one. While we'll stress throughout the book that these guidelines are not strict rules, and that they can and should be customized to fit your particular audience, there are general principles that apply to these models that we, and others we've surveyed in the industry, have found to work effectively in practice. The objects that are included in a HDM are described below.

Concept: A concept is represented as a noun that has meaning to the business. In the HDM, we create an inventory of the words, terms, and concepts used by the business with clear definitions for each. In creating this inventory, it is helpful to think of Who, What, Where, When, Why, and How? For example:

Who?	Employee, Customer, Student, Vendor
What?	Product, Service, Raw Material, Course
Where?	Location, Address, Country
When?	Fiscal Period, Year, Time, Semester
Why?	Transaction, Inquiry, Order, Claim, Credit, Debit
How?	Invoice, Contract, Agreement, Document

A concept is usually shown on the diagram as a box, with its name at the top or center of the box. The reason for this is that HDMs are normally created by data architects who use the HDM to develop the logical data model. The logical data model uses a box to represent an entity.

We'll talk more about notation in Chapter 6, but for now, we'll use the commonly-used box style, as shown in Figure 3.11.

Figure 3.11 – Customer Concept

Customer

Attribute: An attribute is a piece of information about or characteristic of a concept. In a HDM, each concept may have zero, one or more attributes to help impart meaning and understanding. The simplest way to convey what an attribute is would be to give an example. Below are some sample attributes for the Customer concept:

Concept: Customer

Attributes: name, address, gender, customer id, etc.

Attributes are commonly shown inside the box as in Figure 3.12.

Figure 3.12 – Customer Concept with Sample Attributes

Customer

customer id
name address

You might be wondering why there is a line separating customer id from the rest of the attributes. This indicates that customer id is an 'identifying' attribute, which means that you can uniquely identify a particular customer using it. There might be two customers with the same name, for example, but they should each have their own customer identifier.

Do you show attributes on a HDM?

In a survey of data management professionals, 51% reported showing attributes on a HDM. [1]

As you can see, getting into this level of detail in the HDM can sometimes confuse the ultimate goal of providing detail on the definitions and interrelationships of business concepts.[1] For this reason, attributes are considered ***optional*** on the HDM. If they help convey the meaning of a concept, or if clarification of the meaning of a concept is needed, they should be included.

Here's an example of how using attributes might help explain the meaning of a concept. Let's go back to the example in Chapter 2 where we used a high-level data model to help clarify the meaning of 'customer'. In that example, rather than starting by asking users for a definition, we could have started instead by asking them to list some defining attributes of a customer. A customer has a name and address, for example. Everyone we spoke with agreed on that. The Sales organization also listed gender. When the Manufacturing organization saw this, they were confused—all of the customers that they dealt with were corporations—they did not work with individual people and a corporation could not be male or female. By listing the attributes, we were able to arrive at differences in meaning. For Sales, a customer was *an individual* who has purchased a good or service. For Manufacturing, a customer was *a corporation* who has purchased a good or service. This difference could affect how reports are formatted and how billing is handled, for example. It is important to capture the distinctions early in the design cycle. Figure 3.13 shows an

1 Hoberman, Steve. "What's a Good Name for the High-Level Model?" DMReview. 1 Dec. 2008.

example of using attributes to help clarify the meaning of a concept.

Figure 3.13 – Using Attributes to Clarify Meaning

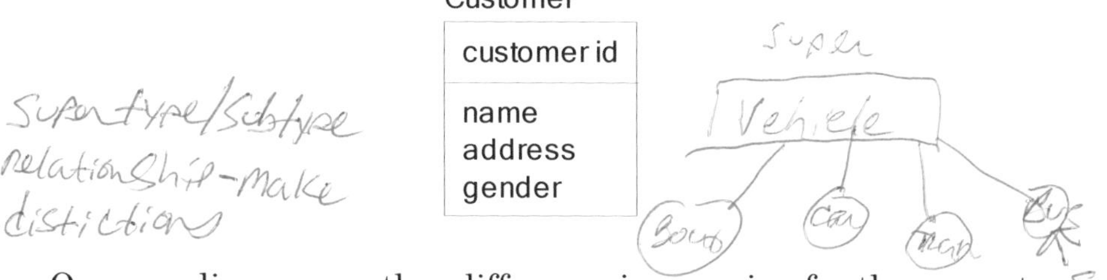

Once we discover another difference in meaning for the concept 'customer', how do we resolve it? In the previous example, we determined that there were really two separate concepts: customer and prospect, so we represented two concepts with different names on our diagram. In this case, however, both customer and prospect are still valid definitions for customer, but we need to represent the difference between individuals and corporations that are either customers or prospects. A technique that helps convey differences such as this is a supertype/subtype relationship. Let's start with an 'official' description and then use an example to help describe what this is.

Supertype/Subtype: Supertypes and Subtypes are a mechanism for grouping objects with similar (but not identical) characteristics. The supertype is the 'master' and contains the attributes and relationships that are shared by all of the subtypes. A subtype is a variation of the supertype and may have some of its own distinct characteristics. For example, let's take a supertype of vehicle, defined as a means of carrying or transporting something. Subtypes would include automobile, airplane, train, and motorcycle.

In the customer example, we determined that a customer can be either an individual or an organization. Different information might be stored about a corporation (e.g. corporate tax id) than for an individual (e.g. gender), and different rules might apply to each. But they are both still customers and there are certain characteristics and rules that apply to all customers. We represent this by creating a supertype concept named 'Customer' and two individual subtypes of 'Corporation' and 'Individual', as shown in Figure 3.14.

Figure 3.14 – Using a Supertype/Subtype Relationship

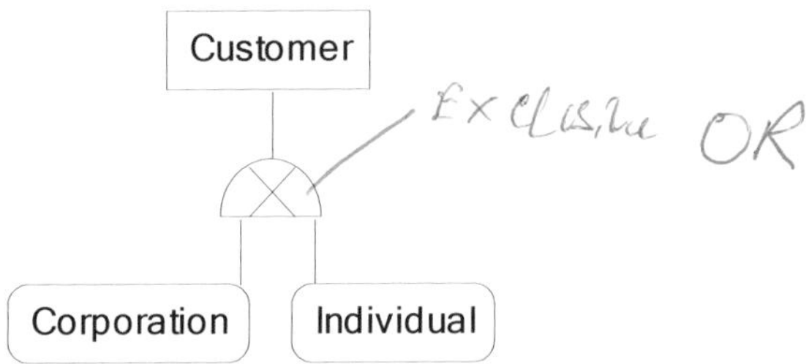

Without any explanation of the notation, you can probably figure out that this diagram is showing that a customer can be a corporation or an individual. That's the goal of a good high-level data model—it should be intuitive to a non-technical person with little or no explanation. The half-moon symbol in the center of the graph with an 'X' in its center is one way to represent a supertype/subtype relationship:

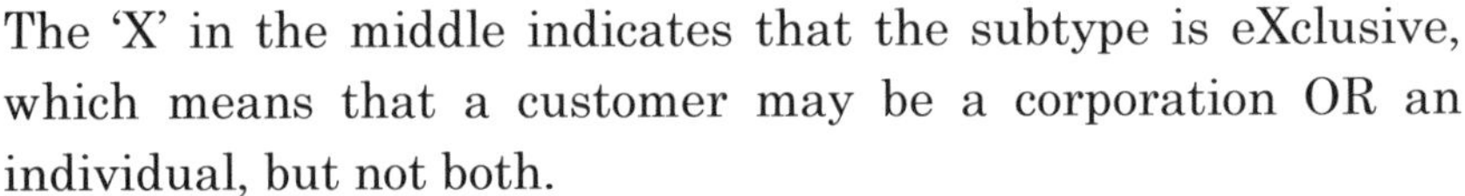

The 'X' in the middle indicates that the subtype is eXclusive, which means that a customer may be a corporation OR an individual, but not both.

<u>Relationship:</u> While concepts show the NOUNS of a business, relationships are the VERBS. Relationship verbs reflect the business rules of an organization for operational databases. For reporting databases, they show the navigation paths for queries. Again, it's probably easiest to explain this by using some examples. Below are some sample business rule relationships that might be expressed in a data model:

- An employee can work for more than one department.
- A department may have more than one employee.
- A customer can have more than one account.
- Sales are reported monthly.

These may seem like very simple and obvious rules to you. But remember, the definition of what a customer is might have seemed obvious, too, before we started delving deeper and asking different departments and individuals how they used the term. And, like the definitions of concepts/nouns, the definitions of these relationships/verbs are critical to ensuring that the database systems that run an organization work correctly and efficiently.

Let's take the first example: "An employee can work for more than one department." When the original database system was built, the developer assumed that each employee works for a single department. He structured the system in such a way that only a single department name could be associated with each employee. This worked fine for several years, until management wanted to track expenses by department more closely and purchased an expense tracking system. For each business trip, employees were asked to specify which department should be billed. This caused a problem for employees whose job role spanned several departments. A product manager, for example, needed to bill Development for business trips to manage product releases, but needed to bill Sales for business trips to support customers. With the existing database structure, this was impossible.

When management asked for an estimate of what it would cost to correct this, the expense was in the thousands of dollars. Remember the analogy of changing the wings of a plane flying across the Atlantic? These sorts of changes are simple to catch in the design phase, but are extremely difficult to change once the database has been implemented because many operations applications are using them to support mission-critical systems.

So how can a business person help define these rules? The easiest way is to create simple statements like the ones we saw earlier. It's not difficult to build simple data models to express these rules—any good data architect should be able to translate them into a data model. Many tools even support translation between a data model and English-style sentences. Understanding how models with rules are developed will help you structure your thought process to build effective rule sentences.

We've already had some experience building simple data models and have focused primarily on *concepts* and their *definitions,* so far. Now we're ready to add the *rules* to these models by adding *relationships.* Remember that a concept is represented by a box. A relationship is shown as a line that connects the boxes on the diagram. Each relationship should be labeled so that it reads like a verb phrase. Building a data model from a rule is similar to diagramming a sentence. First, take a simple sentence that defines a rule. An example is shown in Figure 3.15.

Figure 3.15 – Sentence Defining a Business Rule

A department can contain many employees.

Let's start by putting a box around the nouns and underlining the verb, as shown in Figure 3.16.

Figure 3.16 – Diagramming a Business Rule

By doing this, the sentence is already starting to look like a data model. Putting it into a data modeling tool makes it look like Figure 3.17.

Figure 3.17 – Showing a Business Rule Sentence as a Data Model

It looks pretty similar, right? But what do those symbols on the line mean? Let's go back to the example that caused the problem in the expense tracking system. The problem revolved around whether an employee could belong to more than one department. 'Cardinality' is the term used to describe the numeric relationships between the nouns on either end of the relationship line. It expresses the 'how many' qualifier in a sentence. Let's go back and circle this qualifier in the original sentence, shown in Figure 3.18.

Figure 3.18 – Expressing Cardinality in a Business Rule Sentence

The cardinality 'Many' is represented as a 'crow's foot' symbol in the data model. It is called a 'crow's foot' because, well, it looks like a crow's foot! Take a look at Figure 3.19 and you'll see what we mean.

Figure 3.19 – Expressing Cardinality in a Data Model

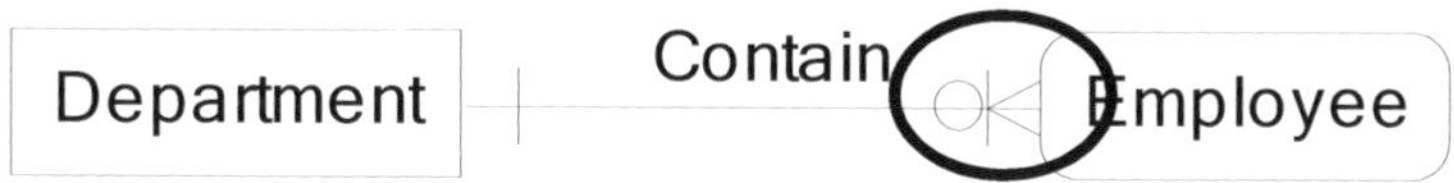

An easy way to decipher cardinality markers is to think of how you might answer the question "How many?" If the answer is "one", you'd hold up one finger. In a data model, this would be shown as follows: ┼ Think of that as an index finger showing 'one' employee. If the answer is more than one, you'd hold up several fingers. Think of the following as several fingers sticking up: ⋲

"Optionality" expresses what can and must happen in a relationship. Note that our sentence says that a department ***can*** contain many employees. In other words, it doesn't have to have any at all, or it can have many—that's what the "O" next to the crow's foot represents::. What this notation is saying is that a department may have no employees (the **O** - optionality), one employee (the **I** - cardinality) or many employees (the crow's foot – also cardinality) and that an employee <u>must</u> belong to one and only one department (the **I** next to Department).

If an employee doesn't have to belong to a department, you can put a 'O' instead of a '1' next to Department. Figure 3.20 shows that an employee can work for only one department or none at all -- a very easy-going company to work for!

Figure 3.20 – Showing 0, 1, or Many Relationships

Another important thing to know about relationships is that, unlike English sentences that read from left to right, relationships read both ways: from left to right and from right to left. If we look at this example again and read from left to right, we'll see that we're enforcing a rule that shows that a department can have more than one employee and an employee can only be in one department. If the business wants to allow an employee to work in more than one department, we would need to change the cardinality on the Department side, as shown in Figure 3.21.

Figure 3.21 – Enforcing Cardinality on Both Sides of a Relationship

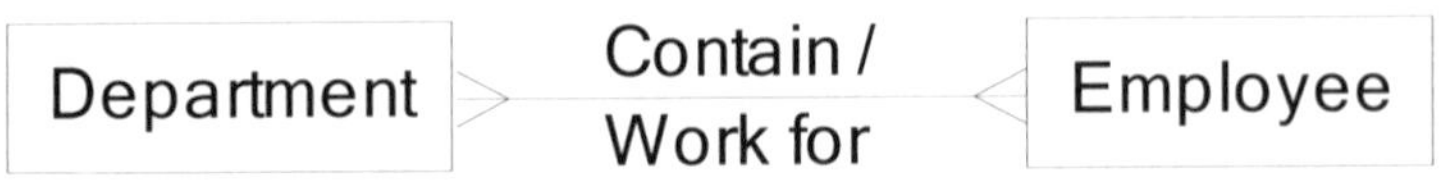

While we were at it, we also added a verb phrase to complete the 'sentence' starting with Employee. So if we read this diagram from right to left, it says: "An Employee must work for many departments", while reading from left to right, we have a rule that says "A Department must contain many employees." As a business person, you could easily create this type of diagram on your own, or simply write out the sentence rules to show to a data architect.

If you do create a diagram similar to the one in Figure 3.21, you will have created what is called a 'many-to-many relationship'. Many-to-many relationships are allowed on the HDM because we are capturing broad business rules. However, on a logical data model, a many-to-many relationship needs to be replaced by more detailed structures which show all of its underlying attributes and relationships.

Tip: Show cardinality and optionality symbols

Cardinality and optionality symbols communicate whether one concept has 'zero', 'one', or 'many' occurrences with the other concept. They help you read the model and add precision. Without showing cardinality and optionality, we are saying there's some relationship between two concepts, but we don't know what it is.

By now, you should have a basic understanding of how the combination of concepts and the relationships between them create the business rules that govern the systems that run an organization. Let's go back to the sample business rules we listed earlier on:

- An employee can work for more than one department.
- A department may have more than one employee.
- A customer can have more than one account.
- Sales are reported monthly.

Now You Try It! Using Concepts and Relationships

In the previous steps, we created an example for the first and second business rules. Now that you have an understanding of the basics of high-level data modeling, try drawing a simple data model for the third business rule:

- A customer can have more than one account.

You can use the simple pen-and-paper approach or create this in your modeling or drawing tool of choice. Once you've given it a try, turn to the answer section in Appendix A to see if you got it right.

Psssst—a thought for this exercise. We mentioned relationships read both ways. Can an account have more than one customer?

Dimensional Models

Now that you have two data models using both concepts and relationships under your belt, let's try modeling the fourth business rule:

- Sales are reported monthly.

The phrase "are reported" should raise a flag in your mind. You'll remember that dimensional models are used to support business intelligence (BI) reporting. In business intelligence applications, data is summarized so that it can be reported on by business users. The information in reports is different from operational data in several ways:

- Operational data is transactional and usually current, with perhaps a few weeks or months of transactions available to the user. Reporting data is retained historically over many years, i.e. Show total profits over the last 10 years.

- Transactional data represents individual transactions. Reporting data is summarized, i.e. Show total annual profits...
- Reporting data that can be measured, such as Total Profit Amount, needs to be 'sliced and diced', or reported on in many different ways or dimensions, e.g. time, region, sales rep, etc.

The differences between operational (relational) and reporting (dimensional) data are reflected in the logical and physical models and the databases that support applications. But there are differences that may be addressed in the high-level data model, as well.

The first difference lies in the definition of concepts. In a dimensional model, concepts normally represent summary data and focus on a single, central concept such as 'sales'. Let's create a definition of sales in our dimensional model so that you can see what we mean:

Sales: represents the Gross Sales Amount, which is the total invoice value of sales, before deducting customer discounts, allowances, and/or returns.

You can see by words such as 'gross' and 'total' that we're dealing with summarized and aggregated data for all customers, rather than the individual customers we were describing in our operational HDM.

The other main difference in a dimensional model is the introduction of the reporting dimensions themselves. A simple pneumonic to help think of this is to remember the phrase: "***BI*** reports ***by*** something" (pronounce both as "bye").

Let's go back to the fourth business rule:

- Sales are reported monthly.

Rephrase it to "Sales are reported ***by*** month." What else are sales reported by? We'll make a "BI" list for Sales:

- Sales ***by*** month
- Sales ***by*** product
- Sales ***by*** region
- Sales ***by*** sales rep

Now that we have the central concept that we want to report on (Sales) and the dimensions by which we want to report (month, product, region, sales rep), we can create a high-level dimensional model, shown in Figure 3.22. In creating dimensional models, we normally place the central concept on which we want to report in the center. The dimensions by which we want to 'slice and dice' the reports are placed in a fan-like structure around this central reporting concept. You'll notice that the result looks a bit like a star, which is why these types of models are often called 'star schemas'.

Figure 3.22 – High-Level Dimensional Data Model for Sales Reporting

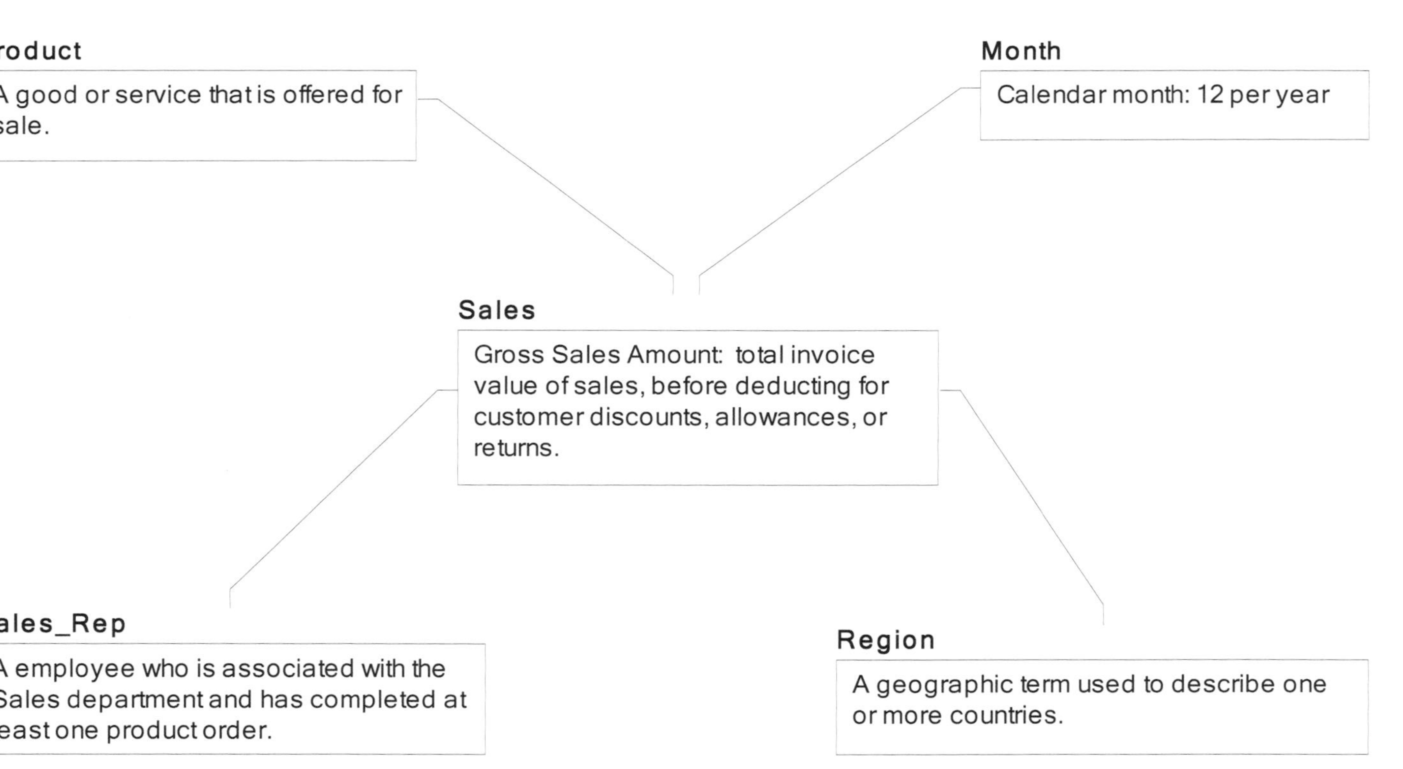

You may also notice that the relationship lines don't have the 'crow's feet' cardinality markers. In dimensional data models, the relationships represent how an application will access data from the database (navigation paths), not business rules, so cardinality offers limited value.

Now You Try It! Creating a High-Level Data Model for BI Reporting

Let's say you work in Human Resources and your company is implementing a new employee salary and benefit reporting system. IT asks you for your requirements. You can impress them by sending them a well-formed dimensional model.

Your report needs to show your company's total salary spending by region. You also want to know which managers are paying their employees the most. And you'll want to see which roles in the organization make the most money. Create a high-level data model for this reporting system. Don't worry about entering definitions for the concepts at this point—just show the concepts that you need to report on and report by. (Hint: this will be a three-sided star). You can compare your result to the one in Appendix A.

Some Important Terms

Before we leave the detailed description of high-level data models, let's define some of the terms that have been mentioned and that will be used throughout the book.

- **Forward/Reverse Engineering:** The process of translating information from one model level to another. The most common use of this term is from the physical data model to an actual database implementation, but it is relevant to all model levels. For instance, you can 'forward engineer' a logical data model from a high-level data model.

- **Impact Analysis:** The process of assessing the impact of a change. For example, if we change the definition of a particular concept, what items in the other model levels or physical implementations will be affected? Impact analysis spans more than just data and data models. It can also show how programs, people, process, etc. are affected. For the purposes of this book, we'll concentrate on the data modeling aspects of impact analysis.
- **Linking:** Creating a relationship between an object in one model level with an object in another.
- **Metadata:** Metadata is the contextual information about your data. Much of the textual information that business people add to a high-level data model would be considered metadata, such as: the description or definition of a concept, the owner of that concept, etc. Metadata also consists of the relationships or context of a concept with other objects. For example, the fact that the customer concept is used by the Sales department or is implemented in a particular database table is also considered to be metadata.

See? Building a high-level data model doesn't have to be complicated. In a HDM you are describing a business, not a database, so you don't need any technical specifics. To build a HDM, you need to start simple, add detail in layers and use a consistent set of methods so that everyone learns what to expect. The HDM process is all about communication! A HDM is not simply an LDM without the attributes; it's a model level that clearly expresses business concepts and rules in a way that both business people and technical people can understand.

Now that you have the basics under your belt, let's move on to the design aspects of modeling. Concept names, definitions, and relationships are critical to capture on an HDM. And along with this comes making the HDM easy for someone to read and interpret.

Key Points

- There are four levels of data models: very high-level (VHDM), high-level (HDM), logical (LDM), and physical (PDM)
- A VHDM shows the purpose, usage, scope, audience, or context of information
- A high-level data model (HDM) describes the major data concepts and rules of the business to facilitate discussion between data architects and business users
- Logical data models show the rules that govern data and the relationships between data objects
- Physical data models represent the translation of the logical data model into the physical structure of a particular database or application
- Relational models are used for describing operational data and dimensional models are used for reporting purposes
- At the VHDM and HDM levels, it is key to balance precision with flexibility to facilitate communication, while at the same time capturing the correct rules and definitions
- While precision of language is important, it's also important that your language and approach be appropriate for your audience to make sure that information is communicated effectively

CHAPTER 4
Layout and Formatting Tips for High-Level Data Models

"A picture is worth a thousand words", as they say, and it is important that the layout and formatting of your HDM be intuitive and easy to understand. An HDM should read like a good book, as shown in Figure 4.1.

Figure 4.1 – A Data Model Should Read Like a Book

Concepts

Place the main concept in the center of the diagram. The HDM should have a main concept as its focus, such as Customer or Order. To keep the model intuitive, place this concept at the center of the diagram, with the supporting concepts around it. For example, if you're developing a Customer HDM, it might look something like Figure 4.2.

Figure 4.2 – Customer Concept as the Center of the Customer HDM

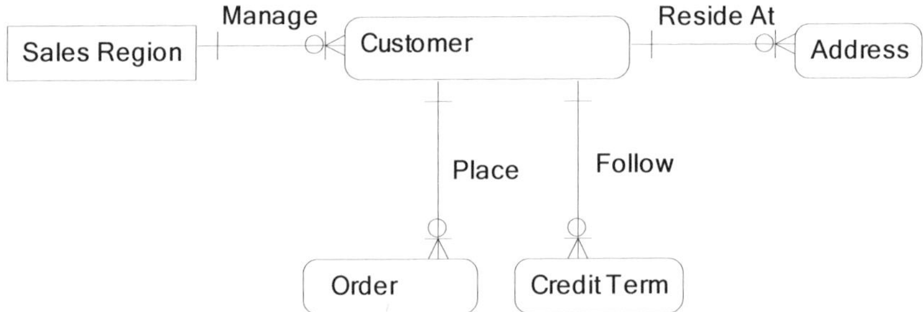

Or if you were developing an Order-centric HDM, it might look something like the model in Figure 4.3. The same Customer concept is used in both models, but in the Order HDM, it is not the main focus—Order is.

Figure 4.3 – Customer Object on Order HDM

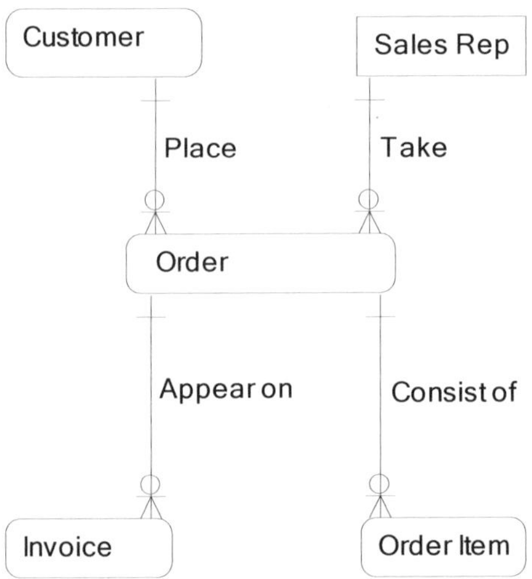

Place Supertypes on Top. If you've defined supertypes and subtypes in your model, make sure that the supertype is on the top with the subtypes below it. Readers intuitively read from top to bottom. See Figure 4.4 for an example.

Figure 4.4 – Place Supertypes Above Subtypes

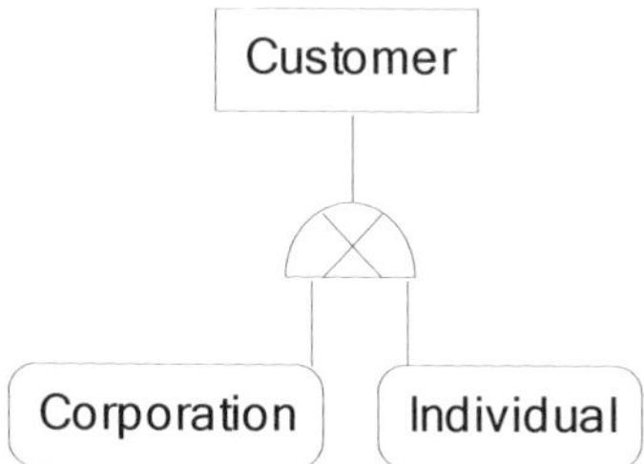

Place Child Concepts Below Parents. Parent concepts are on the one side of a relationship and child concepts are on the many side. So if an order contains many order lines, order line should appear below order.

Show Definitions Where Possible. Concept definitions are critical to the HDM. If it doesn't make the model too difficult to read, they should be displayed in the object boxes. When presenting to or reviewing a model with business users:

- If the number of concepts is small, it is a good idea to show definitions inside of the concept boxes on the model. If the number of objects gets too large, this may be distracting or cause the model to look too crowded.
- If the focus of a review of the model is on the definitions of the concepts, definitely show them. If you are trying to highlight the relationships/rules, it might make sense to hide them so they don't distract from the main purpose.

- In ALL cases, the definitions of the concepts should be documented and reviewed to gain consensus. Definitions should be documented in the model, whether they are displayed on the diagram, or in a document, spreadsheet, web page, etc.

Relationships

Always Show Verb Phrases. Remember, the relationship lines in your HDM are the 'verbs' in your sentence. If you said "My friend _____ the wall", no one would understand you. They'd wonder if your friend had climbed the wall, walked into the wall, or what? Similarly, the rules in your model will not be easy to understand if verb phrases are not shown on the diagram.

Make sure that the relationship line does not cover the verb phrase and that the text is clearly readable. Many modeling tools automatically place the text crossing the relationship line, as shown in Figure 4.5.

Figure 4.5 – Default Text Placement for Verb Phrases

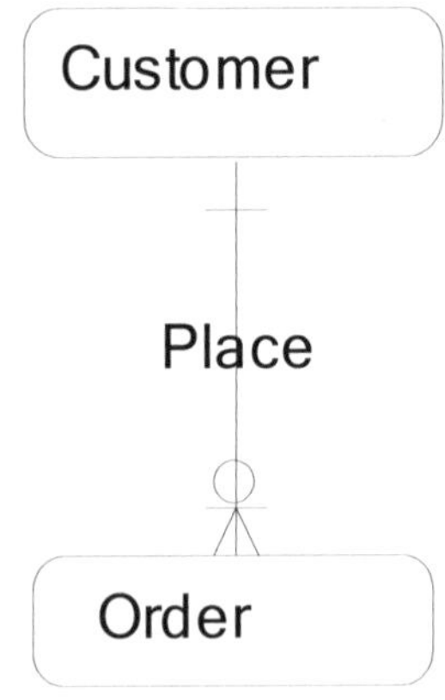

Most tools also let you change this default position to make it more readable, as shown in Figure 4.6.

Figure 4.6 – More Legible Placement for Verb Phrases

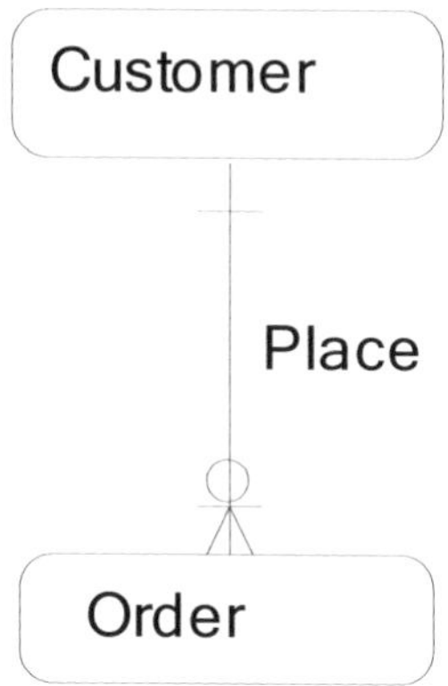

Relationships are read clockwise, so make sure the verb is on the side of the line that reads properly. In Figure 4.6, the verb is placed so that the rule reads "Customer may place one to many Order(s)". If the verb was placed on the other side, it would read "Zero, one to many orders must place one customer" – a nonsense phrase.

When laying out your data model,

- Minimize relationship line length
- Minimize the number of direction changes a relationship line makes
- Minimize the number of relationship lines crossing each other

Other Tips for Effective Model Layout

Here are some other tips to make your HDM as readable as possible.

USE COLOR, FONT, AND WHITE SPACE EFFECTIVELY

If you have access to a color printer, color on a data model can be very effective in making the model more readable.

Following are some options for using color. Try them or come up with your own—there are no rules, so use what works best for you.

- Keep the boxes white and make the background a color, such as a shade of gray
- Draw a rectangle around one or more boxes that make a logical group and color this rectangle
- Color a box that you want to highlight
- Make key concepts larger to stand out more on the model
- Use color, font and box sizes to emphasize things like entity importance, model issues, integration issues, definition issues, etc.
- Don't be afraid of empty space on your model, it adds to legibility

> Color should not be the only method used to convey meaning. I once worked with a color-blind coworker who consistently created presentations and models in shades of beige, or who would create models with a bright green background and florescent yellow objects. To him, it was the contrast that was important, not the colors, and to the audience the result was often painful! (- Donna)
>
> Keep in mind that everyone who will be receiving a soft copy of the model may not have a color printer, so make sure that whatever you do is effective in black and white, too.

KEEP THE HDM TO ONE PAGE WHENEVER POSSIBLE

Simplicity and brevity are the keys to success here. If your model spans more than one page, ask yourself:

- Did I define my subject area, business area, or application too broadly? Should I focus the information in this model on a smaller subset of the business?
- Do any of the concepts express the same idea? Am I using redundant terms for the same thing?
- Should I just use smaller font so that I can fit more stuff onto one page? (We're kidding! ***Never*** do this!)

FORMATTING TIPS FOR DIMENSIONAL MODELS

Dimensional models represent reporting options for summarized data. For these models:

- Place the concept on which you want to report in the center
- Place the concepts by which you want to report radiating around the center, like a star

DON'T BE AFRAID TO USE NON-TRADITIONAL FORMATS

In building a high-level data model, as long as the core concepts are correct, you can be creative in using different methods of getting the point across to the business audience. For example:

- Use pictures in your model instead of a box (e.g. picture of a customer, product, etc.)
- Translate business rules into English-friendly sentences and put them in a document or spreadsheet format
- Publish business definitions on the company's intranet site

Now You Try It! Understanding High-Level Data Models

Now you should be ready to build and understand simple high-level data models on your own. The following examples will help you get started.

Example 1

1. Take the model in Figure 4.7 and turn it into sentences.

Figure 4.7 – Model Representing a 'Sentence'

2. Turn this sentence into a model:

A child may only eat one ice cream cone. If the child does eat an ice cream cone, he will not share it.

Example 2

What's wrong with the formatting of the model in Figure 4.8? It was developed to explain the Sales information requirements to the marketing team.

Figure 4.8 – Badly-Formatted Model

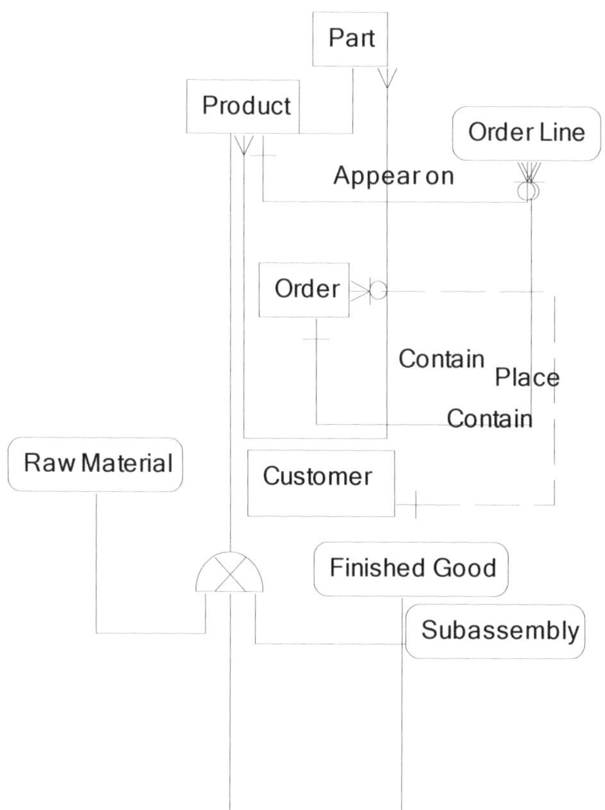

Key Points

- Proper model layout helps increase the communication ability of your model
- Try to keep high-level data models to one page whenever possible
- It's OK to bend the rules and use creative formatting in a high-level data model as long as the concepts you are trying to convey are communicated effectively

CHAPTER 5
What is in a Name?

There are many names floating around in the industry for the high-level data models and there is no absolute consensus on any of them. We've created a matrix in Table 5.1 to map some of the commonly-used names in the industry with the VHDM and the HDM.

Table 5.1 – Commonly-Used Names for the VHDM and HDM

Very High-Level Data Model (VHDM)	High-Level Data Model (HDM)
Enterprise Data Model	Conceptual Data Model
Contextual Data Model	Subject Area Model
C-Level View	Business Data Model
'Picture'/ 'PowerPoint'	'One-Pager'

In a recent survey of data professionals, the most popular names for the high-level models included[2]:

Conceptual Data Model	59%
Subject Area Model	12%
Business Data Model	10%
Enterprise Data Model	6%
Other names:	13%

[2] Hoberman, Steve. "What's a Good Name for the High-Level Model?" DMReview. 1 Dec. 2008.

Notable among the responses was the general consensus that few people were happy with the name they were using. The survey didn't make a distinction between a very high-level data model and a high-level data model, so the responses depended on each person's interpretation of what 'high-level' meant. Because of the dissatisfaction with existing names, and since there was little consensus on a common name for the high-level data models, we decided to distinguish them by using the more generic terms of Very High-level Data Model (VHDM) and High-Level Data Model (HDM).

Since these models are targeted at a business audience, too technical a name might be off-putting to them. The 'conceptual' label, in particular, bothered many respondents because it implies an 'in-the-clouds', academic view which seemed vague. It's hard enough to justify much of the work done by IT to a business person. Telling them that you're building a conceptual model doesn't help— 'conceptual' implies inaction and theory.

The term 'high-level' is commonly used by both the business and IT alike. It has a consistent meaning to most individuals and organizations we surveyed. "Let's start at a high-level, and then drill down into more detail" is an acceptable way to begin a project, as we saw in the earlier house-building example.

Despite all of this discussion around a suitable name for the high-level data model, you may never use the terms VHDM or HDM with your business audience. It makes sense to use terms that have meaning to them. For example, a common type of HDM is the business area or subject area HDM. You may create a Credit HDM, a Sales HDM, etc. So when you're talking to your business sponsor, make sure to call this model the 'Sales Data Model', or the 'Sales Information Model', or the 'Picture that shows the stuff for your Sales BI report'— anything that makes sense to the business user. Remember, the key is to capture their attention, not impress them with your technical lingo.

Key Points

- There are many, varied terms used for high-level data models
- Many people are not happy with the terms used in the industry today
- We suggest the terms Very High-level Data Model (VHDM) and High-Level Data Model (HDM)
- You may end up using different terms with your users, if other terms make more sense to them

CHAPTER 6
Different Modeling Notations

The choice of notation for your VHDM or HDM will directly affect your ability to communicate with your audience. You'll need to consider how the diagram will be used. Will it lead to more detailed logical and physical diagrams for database implementation? Will they be used for software applications/programs that access a database? Or perhaps they're just being used to scope out the types of data that will be needed for a project but won't be developed further? The important thing is whether or not the notation conveys the correct information to its intended audience. Thus, for example, an entity-relationship (ER) model is an ideal choice for data architects with the intention of eventually translating their models into a physical database. This is a common choice for data modeling—so common, in fact, that many of us assume that a data model = an ER model.

But there are other valid choices for data models. UML, for example, is used for application developers who are focusing on classes, not database tables (we'll explain the difference in the UML section). And a business user might prefer to see his or her data constraints in an Excel spreadsheet rather than in a formal model. The good news is that most good modeling tools have the ability to convert, for example, an ER model into a UML class diagram. And there are many third-party software vendors and metadata repository vendors who offer similar translation services. But there are key differences between notations, as well as various 'flavors' within notation types (e.g. Barker, IE, IDEF1X, etc. in the ER world). In the sections that follow, we'll highlight some of the benefits and drawbacks of using particular notations for a high-level data model.

NOTE: While many modeling notations are valid, this book uses Entity-Relationship modeling using the Information Engineering (IE) notation.

Entity-Relationship (ER) Modeling

As we've mentioned, entity-relationship (ER) modeling is one of the most common formats for data models. This style of modeling has been around since the 1970s. A wide range of tools have emerged to support this notation and the generation of physical databases from it. The availability of robust tools to generate databases on a variety of platforms may be the biggest reason for choosing ER as a modeling style.

ER modeling was created for the purpose of describing data and creating databases. Based on relational algebra, ER modeling is well-suited for describing the logic around data and information. Since most database designers use this notation for their logical and physical database designs, it is a natural extension to use this same notation for high-level data models, as well. The benefit of being able to 'link' the various modeling levels is an important one (see Chapter 11 for more on linking). However, this close association with the physical design can also be a drawback, as technical information is apt to find its way into the high-level data model. As we've stressed previously, it's important to keep the high-level model focused on business-related information and free of technical design constructs.

Although we've referred to ER as a single notation, there are many 'flavors' of ER modeling within this notation family. Each has unique ways of expressing relational constructs, with some more intuitive to the business or non-technical user than others. Following is a brief overview of some of the benefits and drawbacks of using a particular ER flavor to describe information constructs to the business. Note that this discussion will not be an exhaustive comparison of the many ways in which these notations differ in describing physical database design—we will only focus on those constructs that appear in high-level data models, such as how simple concepts and relationships are shown, how cardinality is represented, and how supertypes and subtypes are displayed, for example.

Information Engineering (IE)

The Information Engineering (IE) notation has been used in the examples we've shown so far, so it should be familiar to you. Like many ER notations, it uses a box-and-line paradigm to express concepts and relationships. One of the nice features of IE that makes it readable to business users is the use of the 'crow's foot' notation to express cardinality. The diagram in Figure 6.1, for example, shows a many-to-many relationship between employee and department.

Figure 6.1 – Simple High-Level Data Modeling Using IE Notation

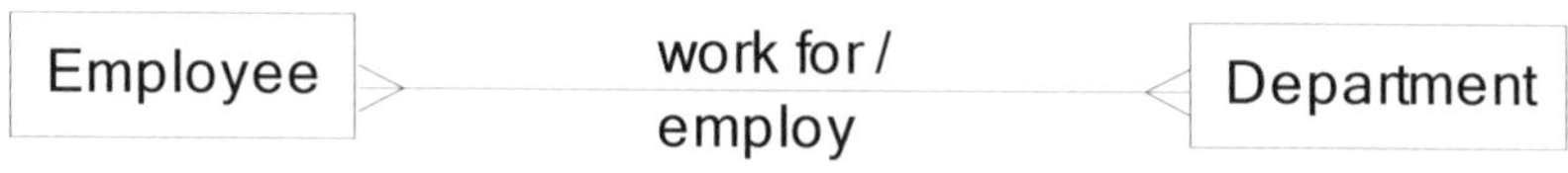

Supertype/Subtype relationships are also fairly intuitive, as shown in Figure 6.2.

Figure 6.2 – Showing Subtypes Using IE Notation

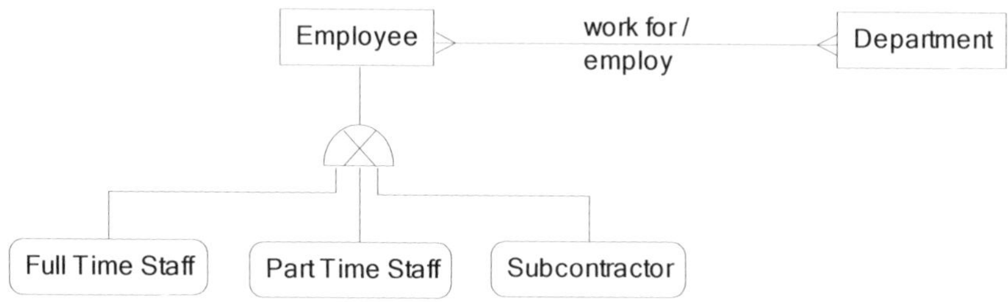

In our experience, business users have found this notation, especially with the addition of verb phrases on the relationship lines, to be easy to understand with minimal training or explanation required.

IDEF1X

The Integrated Definition for Data Modeling (IDEF) is popular with government institutions, and was originally developed by the US Department of Defense. This notation is in many ways similar to the IE notation, with its use of the box-and-line paradigm to show concepts and relationships. The main difference that is relevant to high-level data models is the way in which cardinality is shown. Instead of the 'crow's foot' notation, a solid dot is used to show multiplicity in a relationship. For example, Figure 6.3 shows how the example from Figure 6.1 would be shown using IDEF notation.

Figure 6.3 – Many-to-Many Relationship Using IDEF Notation

In our experience, this style of displaying cardinality is less intuitive to the average reader, although business users can get used to it with a bit of explanation.

Supertypes and Subtypes are also represented using a slightly different symbol, but are, for the most part, shown in a similar fashion to IE. An example is shown in Figure 6.4.

Figure 6.4 – Subtypes Using IDEF Notation

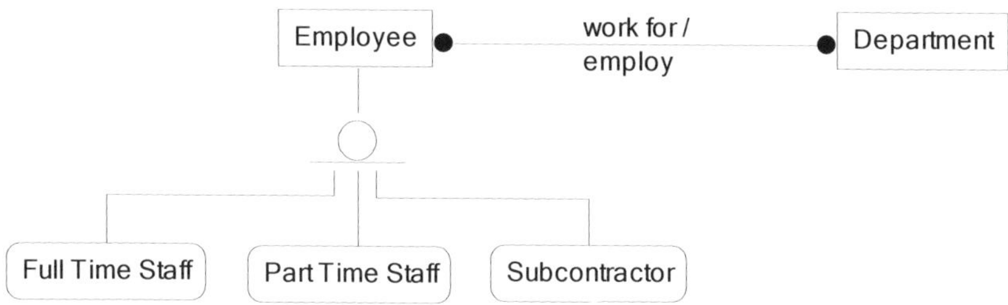

While IDEF notation can be used successfully with a business audience, particularly government clients who might be familiar with the notation, we've found that the notation is less intuitive, particularly because of the way cardinality is expressed.

Barker Notation

The Barker Notation is another popular format for creating high-level data models and is intuitive to the average layperson. Cardinality is shown using the "crow's foot notation", similar to IE in Figure 6.1. As we've mentioned previously, this method of expressing cardinality has proven to be easily understood by a wide range of audiences.

One feature of the Barker notation that is particularly appealing to a non-technical audience is the way supertype/subtype relationships are expressed using a 'box-in-box' format. Figure 6.5 shows the Employee supertype/subtype relationship from previous examples in Barker Notation.

Figure 6.5 – Subtypes Using Barker Notation

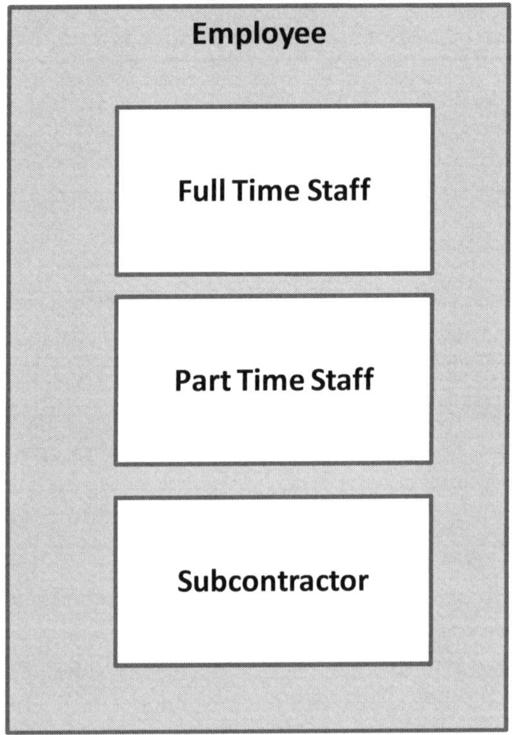

This box-in-box notation is similar to what a business user might create in PowerPoint, and is a visually clean way of showing subtypes. With creative use of color, business users might not know that this is an 'official' data model at all!

UML Modeling

The Unified Modeling Language (UML) notation was designed to be a comprehensive standard for a wide variety of design goals. The UML has a variety of diagram types such as use case diagrams, component diagrams, class diagrams, etc. Business users might be most familiar with use-case diagrams. They may even have created some of these diagrams on their own, using stick figures to depict actors in a particular process, for example. With its wide range of diagram types, object types, etc., understanding the UML can be overwhelming to the average user. The notation caters to application development and the development of runtime code (i.e. not databases), so it is most commonly used by application developers or to communicate with them.

The diagram type most applicable to data and information is the class diagram. For simplicity's sake, a class is analogous to a concept on a high-level data model. A key difference, however, is that an entity-relationship diagram describes the relationships among data, while UML describes the interactions between data and process. The majority of differences will not affect the high-level data model, but they will become a consideration when translating the high-level data model into a technical implementation.

An ER diagram creates the constructs for ***storing information*** in a database, while a UML diagram creates the constructs for ***running software applications/programs*** that use the information stored in the database. So in choosing the notation for your high-level data model, the technical use of the model is an important consideration. If your objective is to create a physical database, an ER model is ideal; if your main goal is to describe information used in programs coded by application developers, UML is a better choice. Most UML tools generate procedural code in a wide variety of languages such as C++, Java, etc. Most ER tools generate database definition code for database platforms such as Oracle, Sybase, Microsoft SQL Server, etc. While most good UML and ER tools can translate their models between notations, the type of detailed modeling you're going to be doing and the intended audience should influence your choice of UML versus ER notation.

The high-level ER data model in Figure 6.1 expressed as a UML class diagram would look like the example in Figure 6.6.

Figure 6.6 – High-Level Data Model Using a UML Class Diagram

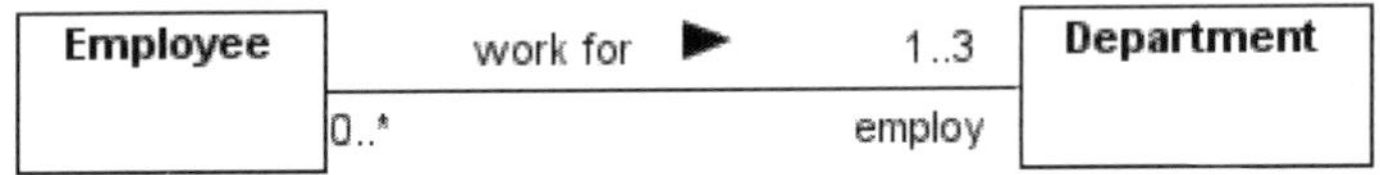

You'll notice the box-and-line notation is similar to ER modeling, but cardinality is expressed differently. This is one area where UML is more intuitive and precise for a business user. Where the IE notation allowed us to show a '1-to-many' relationship, for example, UML allows us to use actual numbers to express cardinality (multiplicity, in UML terms). This diagram shows that a department can employ 0 or more employees. The notation '0..*' is a fairly clear representation of that. The diagram also shows that an employee can belong to 1, 2, or 3 departments, but not 4. That precision is not available in a standard ER diagram.

Verb phrases are also clearly shown, and the ability to include directional indicators is helpful for adding clarity to a high-level data model. For example, it is easy to see in this diagram that an Employee works for a Department, not the other way around.

In UML, supertype/subtype relationships are represented by the concept of 'generalization', which looks very similar to the IE and IDEF ER styles, as shown in Figure 6.7.

Figure 6.7 – Supertype/Subtypes Using UML Generalization

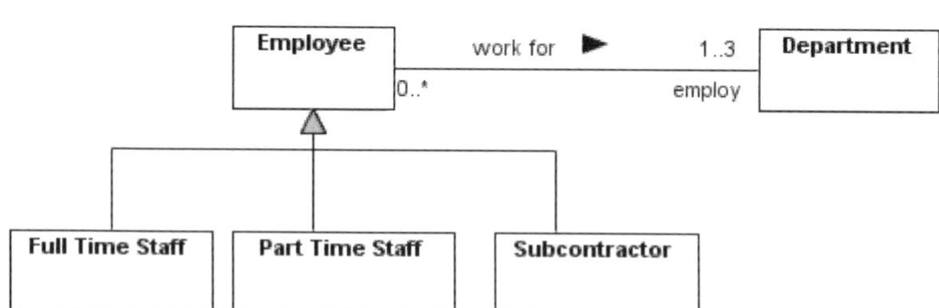

So while there are many differences between UML and ER notations at the physical implementation levels, for a high-level data model, either notation can be used. For some, UML may be a more intuitive format than ER for a high-level data model.

Object Role Modeling (ORM)

Object Role Modeling (ORM) is very different from the other notations we've discussed because ORM was designed primarily for high-level data models. The notations we've already discussed were built for lower-level technical data models and have been adapted for the high-level data model. Let's walk through some of the basics of ORM.

ORM places emphasis on defining core facts of the business that derive the high-level data model. As with our examples for ER modeling in Chapter 3, it is often helpful to create sentences that describe the basic facts. ORM places great emphasis on using actual data samples to express facts. For example, rather than state:

- An employee works for a department

ORM facts would include data samples to read something like:

- An employee John A. Smith works for the Accounting Department
- An employee Jane Q. Doe works for the Sales Department

Using sample data set values early in the high-level data model design process is a good way to ensure that business users and IT are on the same page. By seeing actual examples of real-world data, the ORM diagrams will make more sense to them.

An ORM diagram with sample data is shown in Figure 6.8. Note that the data samples are not officially part of the diagram syntax, but are often included for clarity for the business audience.

Figure 6.8 – HDM Diagram Using ORM

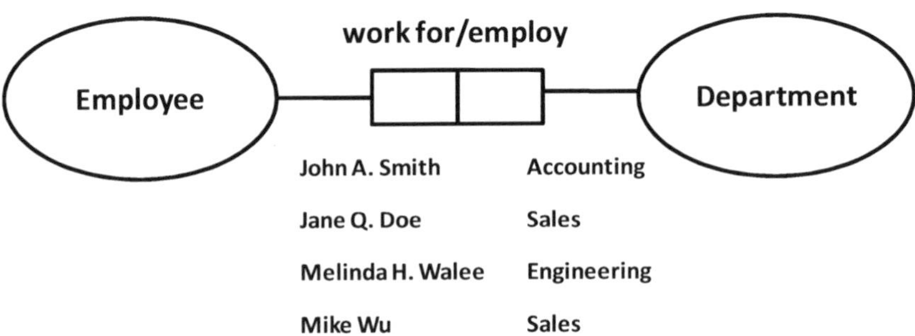

While ORM diagrams can be transformed into detailed logical and physical data models, their focus is on high-level facts and concepts, not on detailed design issues such as attributes, entity/table design, etc. This separation-by-design from the detailed logical and physical models can be seen as both a positive and a negative.

"Natural-Language" Modeling

Translating business rules from a data model into English sentences, e.g. "An employee can belong to only one department" is a helpful way to communicate with a business user. "Natural-Language" modeling also implies precision in phrasing these sentences, so that the translation to and from data modeling symbols produces no loss of information.

Key Points

- There are many different notations that can be used to describe a high-level data model
- Entity Relationship diagrams with IE or IDEF notation are the most commonly-used among data architects
- UML diagrams are popular with application developers
- ORM is a notation aimed at the high-level model user
- Natural language modeling can be used if concepts are accurately conveyed
- Many notations are valid and the key is to use the notation that is most intuitive to your audience

---

CHAPTER 7
How High-Level Data Modeling Fits With Other Data Initiatives

Most organizations today are in some stage of developing large, cross-department data-related initiatives. In this Information Age, data is a strategic differentiator – a retail organization that has a strong vision around its customer information is a step ahead of its competitors. Many of the buzzwords surrounding data-related initiatives are common in both business and IT circles: master data management, business intelligence, data governance, etc. But what do these really mean and how can a high-level data model help with the efforts?

We'll provide a brief overview of several of the hot topics in data management today and discuss how a high-level data model can help with these initiatives. These topics include:

- Business Intelligence and Data Warehousing
- Master Data Management
- Data Governance
- Application Development and Agile Methods
- Enterprise Architecture
- Process Modeling

Many of these initiatives are siloed projects or programs. Programs are large ongoing efforts that have a begin date and, if they are successful, no end date. They require long-term participation from many different sections of the business. Each program contains many bite-sized pieces called projects. A project is a well-defined effort with a begin date, end date and solid deliverables that contribute towards the goal of the program. For example, a data warehouse program can contain many reporting projects such as Profitability and Employee Satisfaction.

Due to the broad scope of program initiatives, very few people (if any) understand the big picture; that is, how the initiative will fully impact the business and how each section of the business, such as Accounting or Sales, will need to be modified to deliver the objectives of the program. What is needed is a simple, yet broad and complete picture showing how concepts cross departments so that the full impact of these large programs can be planned for and prioritized. Do you begin to smell a high-level data model?

One benefit of using a HDM that spans all of these initiatives is integration. The HDM, with its cross-department concept focus, is a perfect communication tool for planning, scoping, impact analysis and project status for each of these large initiatives.

Business Intelligence and Data Warehousing

As we mentioned in the introduction to this chapter, data is a strategic differentiator in today's information-based economy. As organizations realize this, more and more Business Intelligence (BI) initiatives are born. The Data Warehousing Institute defines business intelligence as "The processes, technologies and tools needed to turn data into information, information into knowledge, and knowledge into plans that drive profitable business action."[3] Because of its business focus, BI is one of the initiatives with the greatest involvement of business personnel in the organization. Many business people create their own BI reports.

Included in BI are the software, hardware, network, data models, process models, reports and code to take raw data and

[3] "The Data Warehousing Institute FlashPoint: Excerpt from the upcoming TDWI research report---The Rise of Analytic Applications: Build or Buy?" Data Warehousing Institute Sept. (2002).

turn them into something on which people can base decisions. For example, a manufacturing company can take millions of sales transactions and summarize them into a monthly sales figure. This turns data into information. Monthly sales this year can then be compared against monthly sales last year for the same month, providing knowledge to the user of the information. This knowledge can lead to plans for how much to produce next year, which will hopefully lead to more money, less waste or a better world with more ice cream.

The backbone of any BI initiative is a data warehouse (DW). If a BI report is a flashy sports car, the data warehouse is the engine. A data warehouse is the central storage point for all of the relevant information that is needed for BI reports; and turning data into information is no small feat. A single piece of information on a report, such as 'total sales', can involve the aggregation of hundreds of database tables from multiple geographic and functional areas. And each of the data sources can have different business definitions and physical structures. A major part of the effort of creating a data warehouse is obtaining the big picture of what data exists, how it is defined, and what the end result should look like. This is where a high-level data model can come in handy. See Figure 7.1, which shows how source and reporting applications can complicate the data warehouse program. The reporting applications are often called 'data marts'.

Figure 7.1 – The Data Warehouse is a Great HDM Opportunity

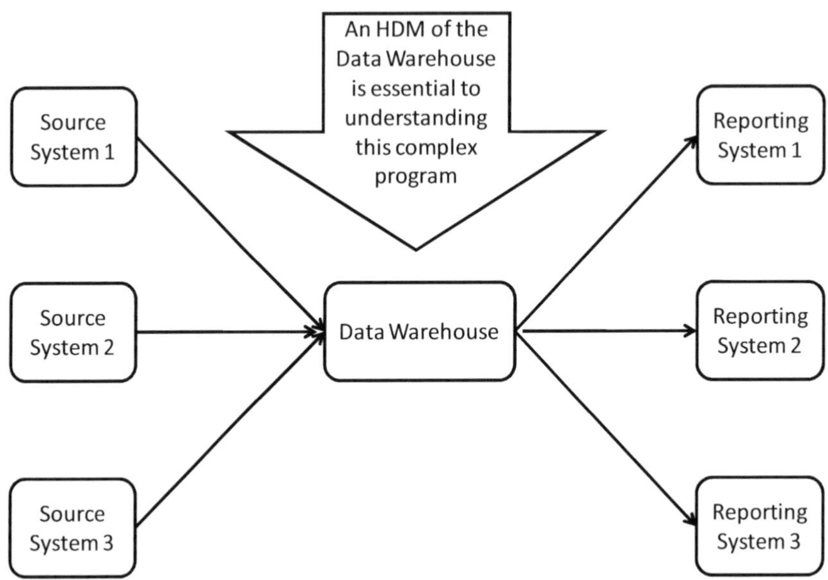

A HDM for a data warehouse provides the following benefits:

Common language. A HDM provides a single agreed-upon set of concepts, definitions and business rules. This language must be consistent across the scope of the HDM. If the scope of the HDM is the data warehouse itself, concepts such as Customer and Gross Sales need to be defined consistently. 'Customer', as defined by Accounting, must be consistent with the Sales Department definition of 'Customer'. The HDM can represent the ideal vision for the data warehouse (e.g. one definition for 'Customer'), and also contain linkages back to the current, more inconsistent environment.

Common language enables the reader of the model to understand where the organization is striving to go, as well as conceptually how to get there from the existing environment. This common language has a direct benefit for the many users of the data warehouse, who can confidently interpret the concepts the same way. Take, for example, this business question: *In what **regions** are **sales** down this **year** compared to the same period last year*? The data warehouse HDM will have a single, agreed-upon definition for all of the terms in bold in this question, thereby increasing the chances of making a profitable business decision based on the response to this question.

Impact analysis. The HDM can be an effective tool for determining overlap and touchpoints. An overlap is when two or more different development teams are impacting the same concept such as when two different development teams are both updating customer information. A touchpoint is when two or more different development teams need to connect with each others' work. For example, when one development team is working on Product and another development team is working on Order, which has a dependency on Product. The link from Order to Product must be managed successfully.

A HDM can represent the entire data warehouse. One of the techniques for effective model layout, such as color, could be used to indicate to management where the touchpoints and overlaps exist for a particular phase of the data warehouse program. For example, a red concept 'Customer' could indicate that at least two development teams are working on this same area for the same release date. A large bold relationship line between Customer and Order could indicate that in this release, there is a touchpoint that exists between these two concepts. The HDM can be updated during the lifecycle of the development effort to indicate successfully managed touchpoints and overlaps, as well as those that are experiencing problems.

Scoping and prioritization. Similar to using color for impact analysis, we can use color to indicate which part of the BI program will be developed first, second, and so on. For example, those concepts shown in green will be implemented as part of Customer Profitability by first quarter next year. In every project status meeting, this BI HDM can be presented to show progress since the last status meeting at a concept level. The HDM therefore, becomes a part of every status document.

Employee education. When new people join the data warehouse team, there is usually a fairly steep learning curve. The new person needs to learn about the system architecture, data architecture, and the business in general. Starting this person off on the first day with a walk-through of the data warehouse HDM can give them a solid, high-level understanding of the area in which they will work -- raising their confidence and reducing the amount of time it takes for them to learn the details. Employee education applies to both the business user who needs a high-level overview of the navigation paths in their reports, as well as the IT team member who needs to understand how their involvement in the project fits in with the whole BI initiative.

Building reports: Business people are often actively involved in building their own BI reports, which has, in part, fueled the growth of this technology. In building a report around 'total sales for product x', it is critical for them to understand the definition of both total sales and product. For example, does 'total sales' include both US and worldwide sales or just US sales? There's a big difference, but it might not be obvious without a clear, published definition. Does product include only finished goods or are raw materials included as well? Again, this could cause a big difference in the interpretation of the resulting number on the report. A high-level data model is a great tool for a business user to use in finding these definitions.

Master Data Management

Master Data Management (MDM), like data warehousing, involves the aggregation of diverse data sources into a single location with common structure and definitions. But while a data warehouse is used for reporting, a master data 'hub' deals also with operational data. Remember the analogy of changing the wings on a moving plane from Chapter 2? Master data management initiatives are particularly difficult because they involve operational data that is in use by the business processes that run the organization.

Master data is any data that is used by and shared across the entire organization. Master Data Management initiatives usually concentrate on the subject areas of information that are used by the majority of applications in a company. Not surprisingly, 'customer' and 'product' are two of the most common candidates for master data management today.

As we've seen, different areas of the organization can have very different names and definitions for the same concept. Customer for example, starts off as a 'Prospect' in the eyes of marketing and may end up as a 'Customer Last Address Unknown' in the eyes of billing. The same actual customer spans the entire organization, however. Remember the example of trying to get a single, consolidated statement from your bank in Chapter 2? A successful master data management initiative around 'customer' would have made it easier to accomplish.

Master data may include Customer, Product and Employee, for example, all of which represent reference data. Reference data is the information that supports the many events of importance to the organization. To a business user, reference data takes the form of drop-downs and other report selection variables. Event-based concepts can also be master data, however. The concept of Gross Sales, if it is relevant across the entire company, would also fit this definition.

In order to use a piece of master data consistently, it must have the same definition and rules across the business. The HDM can be a great starting point to ensure that this consistency exists.

A HDM containing master data concepts provides the following benefits:

- **Consistent use.** Because master data must be used consistently across the business, it must have the same name and definition. A HDM spanning the entire scope of a particular master data concept will ensure this. Customer for example, will have one agreed-upon definition across the business. A recent example is the Professional Petroleum Data Management Association (PPDM) organization's effort to come to agreement on the meaning of a 'Well'. After a huge debate, PPDM's members eventually reached consensus. The terminology, business rules and definitions for 'Well' and related concepts could be documented on a 'Well' HDM that would be available for reference if there are questions on 'Well' metadata.

- **Linkages.** An important item to capture on master data is where it exists within the business. A HDM can provide important linkages back to everywhere a particular master data concept is created, changed or used. An HDM deliverable may be more than just a pretty set of boxes and lines. It can also include a mapping of the sources of and references to the concepts. This linkage at the concept level can be an invaluable starting point for mapping at a data element level. The case study in Chapter 14 has actual examples of linkages.
- **Stewardship.** The HDM can be color-coded or labeled in some other way to indicate who is responsible for a particular business area. "All concepts whose text appears in italics are Bob's responsibility." It can be a great technique for identifying and finding master data owners.

Data Governance

Data governance is currently defined in Wikipedia as: "A quality control discipline for assessing, managing, using, improving, monitoring, maintaining, and protecting organizational information. It is a system of decision rights and accountabilities for information-related processes, executed according to agreed-upon models which describe who can take what actions with what information, and when, under what circumstances, using what methods." In other words, it encompasses the overall management of the availability, usability, integrity, and security of data.

There are four ways data governance is generally managed: by subject area, application, department or geographic boundary, or by a hybrid approach. All of these approaches work, although with different levels of success and resource expenditures. The correct data governance approach for your organization will depend on your organizational requirements and data resource management maturity.

The easiest approach to implement is generally managing data by department. The most effective approach tends to be by subject area. In practice, most organizations use a hybrid approach. In a hybrid model, the data is managed at a region level by a regional information manager, using local data stewards and local data owners. The informational manager performs the coordinating function among the regional informational managers. Over time, this type of model can mature into a data subject area model. In resource-constrained organizations, it is desirable to implement a subject-oriented or hybrid approach.

Regardless of the approach implemented in your organization, the governance activities are coordinated through a community such as a data governance board or community of practice. These activities include planning, control and supervision, along with the associated processes for conflict resolution, education and awareness, strategic data planning, project oversight and KPI (Key Performance Indicator) monitoring.

A HDM with a broad organization scope provides the following benefits for data governance:

- **Planning.** The HDM is used as the guide for all data governance activities and their associated processes. Each concept on the high-level data model will have a data owner and one or more data stewards. Data owners, stewards and information managers may reside in any part of the organization chart; however their fundamental loyalty and belief structure must belong to the business community rather than the information technology community. Data asset planning is based on the data concepts either within the regional area, or across an enterprise.

- **Accountability.** In more mature organizations, traceability and accountability can be aligned directly within the high-level data model. This can be accomplished by adding properties to the data modeling tool to capture data governance attributes. It can also be accomplished using techniques mentioned earlier, such as the use of color or font. For example, Bob is accountable for Customer information and his color is 'red'.

Application Development and Agile Methods

The gap between application development, which often uses Unified Modeling Language (UML), and database development is often the largest one to bridge—even harder than getting business people and data architects to communicate. The need for common definitions is critical to ensuring that the applications being coded are meeting the needs of the business and match the rules and definitions that are defined in the database systems.

Agile means 'quick' and 'adept'. When applied to application development, agile translates into rapid delivery of high-quality software. Agile usually means there are many project-focused iterations until the project is complete. Proponents of agile methods say the project-focused approach produces high quality results in much less time than a typical software development methodology. Opponents of agile say the focus of agile is on the project at the expense of the program, meaning the enterprise perspective and 'big picture' are not given the attention they require. This is not a book on agile pros and cons, so we'll leave the discussion at that. However, if a business or IT member of an agile development team feels the enterprise view will suffer, he or she can create an enterprise HDM.

A HDM provides the following benefits in an application development and/or agile environment:

- **Enterprise fit.** Because HDMs take a relatively short amount of time to build, they will not slow down an agile project. An agile project can have its own HDM which can be compared to the enterprise HDM to ensure consistency. This way, at least at a concept level, the agile project is delivering part of the 'big picture'. Issues that arise at this level can be tracked at the more detailed data element level to make sure the project stays on track.
- **Managing scope.** Agile projects are typically small in scope. Having a HDM of the agile project as well as an enterprise HDM can help ensure that only the required scope is delivered. New concepts that come up in requirements sessions that are on the enterprise HDM but not on the agile project HDM can be brought up in management sessions so that the scope and, if necessary, the project timeline can be reevaluated.
- **Communication:** A HDM is not bogged down by technical specifics, so some of the gap between application developers and database developers that we referred to can be mitigated by using high-level constructs and user-friendly graphics. Programmers and database developers might get into an argument over the benefits of UML vs. ER diagrams, but it's a lot harder to argue about a graphical smiley-face representing a customer concept, a picture of a wrench to describe a product concept, or a big circle to describe sales information. Making the diagram generic in this way removes some of the cultural barriers between the groups.

Enterprise Architecture

Enterprise Architecture (EA) is a broad initiative that attempts to create a high-level roadmap of an organization's technical infrastructure. It involves not only data, but also the people, processes, hardware, networks, etc. that run an organization and how these different areas interact. A simple way of thinking of EA is that it represents the 'who', 'what', 'where', 'when', 'why', and 'how' of an organization. So while there is a high-level data model showing the 'what' of an organization, there will be a corresponding high-level process model showing the 'how' (explained more in the following section), a high-level organizational diagram showing 'who', etc. A key aspect of the enterprise architect's role is to coordinate the touchpoints and interactions between data and process, or process and people, or hardware and data.

If your organization has an enterprise architecture program, organization, or initiative, chances are that they will be involved with or even have direct responsibility for the creation of the VHDM and HDM.

Process Modeling

As we discussed in the context of Enterprise Architecture, data models describe the 'what' of an organization. Process models, then, describe 'how' an organization runs. They describe the things that have to happen to do business. For example, if we don't have a process to add customers, we won't have any customers in our system. If we don't have processes for taking orders or producing a product, our business won't function. Similar to the levels of data models, process models provide a way of documenting and defining the functions and processes of a business in successively more detail.

To get a clear understanding of how data and process interact, it's important to understand which data concepts are used by a particular process. A common way of showing this interaction is through a CRUD matrix. CRUD is an acronym that indicates what data has been **C**reated, **U**pdated, **R**ead, or **D**eleted by a particular business process. For example, in the CRUD matrix shown in Table 7.1, we can see that customer information is both read and updated by the Sales Order Process. More importantly, we can also see that two processes use the same Customer data: Sales Order and Product Shipment. This is critical when we are assessing the impact of change. If we changed the definition or structure of the Customer concept (and the associated physical structure in the database that supports the process), we might break something in the Product Shipment process if all parties involved aren't aware of the change.

Table 7.1 – Sample CRUD Matrix

	Sales Order	Product Shipment	Manufacturing
Customer	R,U	R	
Product	R	R	C
Invoice		C	

Processes interact with data and process models utilize the data artifacts defined in the data models to represent the interaction. Without attempting to get into any methodology-specific arguments, it's fair to say that good process modeling will define models at similar levels to those defined in data modeling. Table 7.2 provides a summary view of how the levels of process and data models relate to each other.

Table 7.2 – Relationship with Between Process and Data Model Levels

	Very High-Level	High-Level	Logical	Physical
Data	Contains 'big picture' of subjects, context, and some vocabulary	Contains concept terminology, definitions, and rules	Contains technology-independent view	Contains technology-dependent view
Process	Contains highest level processes, and distinguishes functions from processes	Contains key business process steps and dependencies	Contains design of processes, tools, and methods	Contains implementation of screens, applications, and queries

Now You Try It! Using High-Level Data Models in Your Organization's Data Initiatives

1. Which of the initiatives described above are in place at your organization? (Business Intelligence, Master Data Management, Application Development, Enterprise Architecture)
2. What information concepts are common to each of these initiatives? (customer, product, etc.)
3. Create a HDM to describe these concepts.

Key Points

- Many data-related or IT initiatives commonly underway today can benefit from the use of a high-level data model
- Business Intelligence and Data Warehousing can use a HDM to arrive at common concept definitions to improve the quality and accuracy of reporting
- Master Data Management can leverage a HDM to promote the 'single version of the truth'
- Data Governance can benefit from a HDM to help manage and account for data
- Application Development and Agile Methods need to understand a common definition of data concepts as much as 'traditional' data-focused initiatives do
- Enterprise Architecture aligns closely with VHDMs and HDMs as architects assess a comprehensive view of the organization. Data is the 'what' of an enterprise architecture initiative.
- Process Modeling and data modeling linked together achieve an integrated view of how business processes use and access strategic information

CHAPTER 8
Creating a Successful High-Level Data Model

Master the techniques for creating the high-level data model (HDM) in this chapter. Learn the ten-step approach to building the HDM and increase your awareness of a number of factors and constraints that will heavily influence the actual modeling process. These factors and constraints will need to be understood and weighed so that you can wisely choose the modeling approach that best suits your needs—top-down, bottom-up, or a combination of the two as a hybrid approach.

Ten steps to completing the HDM

We've identified ten steps that are required to complete the HDM. Although you can start some of the steps out of sequence, they need to be completed in the order they appear. For example, you might find yourself jotting down stakeholders (Step 2) before identifying the purpose of the model (Step 1). However, you will need to revisit your model stakeholder list after finalizing the purpose of the model.

The ten steps for completing the HDM are:

1. **Identify model purpose**. Determine and agree on the primary reason for having a HDM. Always begin with the end in mind.
2. **Identify model stakeholders**. Document the names and departments of those who will be involved in building the HDM, as well as those who will use it after its completion.
3. **Inventory available resources**. Leverage the results of Step 2 to determine what people will be involved in building the HDM and also identify any documentation that could provide useful content to the HDM.

4. **Determine type of model**. There are four different types of HDMs that we will discuss in this chapter. One of them will need to be chosen based on the purpose of the model and the available resources.
5. **Select approach**. Chose either a top-down, bottom-up, or hybrid approach based on the purpose of the model and the available resources.
6. **Complete an audience-view HDM**. Produce a HDM using the terminology and rules that are clear to those who will be using the model.
7. **Incorporate enterprise terminology**. Now that the model is well-understood by the audience, ensure the terminology and rules are consistent with the organizational perspective.
8. **Signoff**. Require and obtain approval from the stakeholders that the model is correct and complete.
9. **Market**. Similar to introducing a new product, advertise the data model so that all those who can benefit from it know about it.
10. **Maintain**. HDMs require little maintenance, but they do require some. Make sure the model is kept up-to-date.

Let's go through each of these steps in detail.

STEP 1: IDENTIFY MODEL PURPOSE

Before starting any data modeling effort, first identify why the model needs to be built. It is important to remember to focus the purpose of the high-level data model around a business need or process improvement. For example, you're not likely to get much interest from a corporate sponsor by saying that you need $100,000 to "rationalize critical customer data elements". But if, instead, you tell the sponsor that this initiative will help improve the company's marketing program effectiveness by making sure that we have correct customer information, and that all departments are sharing this information for their corporate-wide initiatives, you are likely to get some interest (and funding!). This will be important to remember when we get to the marketing step later on. If you haven't identified the right pain point and solution, it will be impossible to sell the HDM to your audience, no matter what you do.

Underlying every reason for building a HDM is communication. We build data models so that we can ensure everyone has a precise understanding of terminology and business rules. Part of this step is to identify what needs to be communicated and to whom we are communicating it.

One of the fascinating outcomes of this first step is the realization that the model stakeholders see the world very differently from each other. (If they don't see the world differently at this first step, they surely will while building the high-level data model and attempting to agree on a single definition for Customer, for example.) Therefore, they also may have differences of opinion on the purpose of the model. You will find that the same skills that get people from different departments to agree on definitions for terms like Customer are invaluable in Step 1 for gaining consensus on why the model is being built.

Good facilitation skills can never be underestimated in this first step. The skillful facilitator knows when to involve upper management and when to use 'tough love' techniques such as making the bold statement, "No one is leaving this room until we all agree on why we are building this model in the first place!" It is not worth investing time and money in the other nine steps without a clear, agreed-upon reason for the model. That doesn't mean the high-level data model cannot have more than one purpose, but there should be one *primary* purpose for building it.

Once there's consensus on the purpose of the data model and it is documented, we can combine this knowledge with a number of factors, to be discussed shortly, to determine whether a top-down, bottom-up, or hybrid approach is ideal. Matching the right factors with the right modeling approach will dramatically increase the probability of having a successful model.

Here are the most common reasons for building a HDM (remember, communication is the main reason behind each of these):

- **Capture existing business terminology and rules.** The most popular use of the HDM is to gain an understanding of an existing area of the business. We can model a department such as Sales or Accounting, a line of business such as Home Mortgages, or even the entire organization. If the model crosses broad functional areas as in the example of Home Mortgages, it can become a valuable tool for people with different backgrounds and roles to understand and communicate with each other on the same concepts, and agree or debate on issues. The HDM becomes the medium for getting people to agree on whether the concept should be called 'Client' or 'Customer', and then completing the near impossible task of getting people to agree on a single definition for 'Client' or 'Customer'. It also becomes the medium for obtaining agreement on business rules such as "A Customer must own at least one Account."
- **Capture proposed business terminology and rules**. Our businesses continuously try to find ways to improve execution of the day-to-day events that keep us in business. For example, if it takes 5 hours to manufacture a widget, how can we get this down to 4 hours and 30 minutes? Therefore, after understanding existing business terminology and rules, we need to agree on a future state for this same set of terminology and rules. For example, although today "A Customer *must* own at least one Account", tomorrow the business might want this rule to be "A Customer *may* own at least one Account." The term 'must' implies mandatory, whereas in the future the business would like a

Customer to exist without owning an account. Maybe the business would like Customer to include the concept of 'Prospect' or 'Applicant', who do not yet own accounts.

- **Capture existing application terminology and rules**. In the beginning of a project, there is always a period of time where there are large gaps in understanding the existing applications. This may include functionality, terminology and reporting gaps. It may include internally-built applications as well as packaged software such as Enterprise Resource Planning (ERP) applications. It may include both operational and reporting systems. Operational systems, you'll remember, are those that help the business execute transactions and survive, reporting systems are those used to evaluate the business and make strategic decisions. In many cases, understanding an existing application is a prerequisite to building a new application. At one point, we needed to understand part of SAP/R3, so the purpose of the model was to capture the existing application. We deliberately chose terminology and rules that the application used, and not the business. For example, SAP/R3 used the term 'Object' for a concept that the business called 'Customer'. We chose to use the term 'Object' on the model.
- **Capture proposed application terminology and rules**. The HDM is a very good place to start capturing the concepts and business rules for a new application. This way terminology, rules and definitions can be agreed upon prior to detailed project analysis. It will save time, money, and unpleasant surprises further down in the software lifecycle. As with the existing application, this may include functionality, terminology, and reporting gaps. It may include both operational and reporting systems. It may include internally-built applications as well as packaged software such as enterprise resource planning applications.

Table 8.1 summarizes these four reasons using Customer and Account as an example.

Table 8.1 – Communication Example of All Four Reasons for Building a HDM

	Existing	Proposed
Business	"Today an Account can only be owned by one Customer."	"By next quarter, an Account can be owned by more than one Customer."
Application	"In the legacy Account Management system, we call the customer an Account Holder."	"When we migrate to SAP/R3, Account Holder will be represented as Object."

STEP 2: IDENTIFY MODEL STAKEHOLDERS

A HDM stakeholder is someone who will be affected directly or indirectly by the model that is produced during the modeling sessions. There are a number of roles that would be useful in building and using the HDMs. Table 8.2 summarizes these roles and Table 8.3 identifies which roles typically build and use the HDM. As you might expect, when the purpose of the HDM is to capture an existing or proposed section of the *business*, the builders tend to be people who know the business, such as business analysts and business users. Similarly, when the purpose of the HDM is to capture an existing or proposed *application*, the builders tend to be more technical, such as developers and database administrators. The users of the model though, could be anyone from business and/or IT.

First, let's identify some common roles, shown in Table 8.2.

Table 8.2 – Roles Involved in Building the HDM

Role	Description
Application Tester	A person who ensures application functionality is consistent with the business requirements by using the application and trying to find problems.
Architect	An experienced and skilled designer responsible for architecture supporting a broad scope of requirements over time beyond the scope of a single project. The term implies a higher level of professional experience and expertise than an analyst, designer or developer.*
Business Analyst	An IT or business professional responsible for understanding the business processes and the information needs of an organization, for serving as a liaison between IT and business units, and acting as a facilitator of organizational and cultural change.*
Business User	A person who enters information into an application or queries the application to answer business questions and produce reports.
Database Administrator	The IT professional role responsible for database administration, the function of managing the physical aspects of data resources, including database design and integrity, backup and recovery, performance and tuning.*
Data Manager	An IT professional who manages data resources and data activities in support of organization projects and programs.
Data Modeler	A business systems analyst who identifies data requirements, defines data and develops and maintains data models.*

Table 8.2 – Roles Involved in Building the HDM (continued)

Role	Description
Developer	A person who designs, codes and/or tests software. Synonymous with software developer, systems developer, application developer, software engineer, and application engineer.*
Functional Analyst	A person who analyzes and understands the operations of a business function, then identifies the gaps and mappings between business requirements and proposed or existing applications.
Project Manager	A person who manages project resources and activities in order to deliver the agreed-upon project outputs.
Project Sponsor	A person who can make decisions, ensures the project is aligned with strategic goals, overcomes roadblocks and advocates for the project.
Team Lead	A person who manages a team that produces a subset of deliverables for a project.
Technical Analyst	A person who knows how the proposed or existing application works (or will work).
Technical Support	A person who ensures an existing application meets the service level expectations of the user community by solving problems and answering questions.
Trainer	A person who educates application users on how to use the system.

* Quoted from **The DAMA Dictionary of Data Management,** authored by DAMA International, published by Technics Publications LLC, 2008.

> Participation is required from ***both*** business and IT roles for success. I remember one project I worked on where only IT people showed up to build the HDM. As enthusiastic as we all were to build the model and get support for the project, it was a losing effort because without the business, the model lost credibility and the project therefore lost financial support. (- Steve)

Table 8.3 identifies which roles are involved in which functions in the building or usage of the HDM.

Table 8.3 – Model Stakeholder Functions

Role	Builder – Business Focus	Builder – App Focus	User
Application Tester		✓	✓
Architect	✓	✓	✓
Business Analyst	✓		✓
Business User	✓		✓
Database Administrator		✓	✓
Data Manager		✓	✓
Data Modeler	✓	✓	✓
Developer		✓	✓
Functional Analyst	✓	✓	✓
Project Manager		✓	✓
Project Sponsor	✓	✓	✓
Team Lead		✓	✓
Technical Analyst		✓	✓
Technical Support		✓	✓
Trainer			✓

With the exception of the Trainer who can use the model as a teaching aid to explain key application or business concepts to application users or new hires, all other roles can be used as a resource in building the HDM. Those with more of a business-oriented background can help build the business-focused view and those with more of a technical background can help build the application-focused view.

A subset of the builders and users listed in Table 8.3 will be the builders and users of your specific HDM. All or some of those users should also be your stakeholders and are required to sign off on the model. The signoff will be discussed in Step 8.

With the large potential number of participants, all modeling activities must be time-boxed. By dedicating half a day, a day, or a week and using techniques such as meetings with free pizza and ice cream, the HDM can be built successfully.

STEP 3: INVENTORY AVAILABLE RESOURCES

Now that you have identified why you are building the model and who will be involved in building and using it, we need to identify the ***resources*** we will be using. The two types of resources are: people and documentation.

People include representatives from both business and IT. Business people may be management and/or knowledge users. IT resources can span the entire IT spectrum, from analysts through developers, from program sponsors to team leads. From the people side, this step can be as simple as assigning actual people to the builder roles in Step 2. For example, if we are building a HDM of the manufacturing section of our business, Bob, the business analyst who spent 20 years of his career working in the plant, would be an excellent resource to assign as a builder.

Documentation includes systems documentation or requirements documents. Systems documentation can take the form of standard vendor documentation for a packaged piece of software (e.g. SAP/R3 standard documentation or the Customer Relationship Management (CRM) software user guide), or documentation written to support a legacy application. Requirements documents span business, functional and technical requirements and can be an essential input to building the HDM.

STEP 4: DETERMINE TYPE OF MODEL

The purpose of the model from Step 1 aids in determining the type of model to build in Step 4. The HDM needs to be one of four different variations, as shown in Table 8.4.

Table 8.4 – Determining Type of Model

	Relational	Dimensional
Business	Choose when capturing how the business works and there is a need to understand a business area, design an enterprise data model, or start a new development effort.	Choose when capturing how the business is monitored and there is a need to visually capture how the business is going to play with numbers. That is, view metrics at different levels of granularity, such as by Month and Year.
Application	Choose when capturing how an application works and there is a need to understand an existing or proposed application, or start a new development effort.	Choose when capturing how the business is monitored through a particular application. The application allows users to view metrics at different levels of granularity, such as by Month and Year.

The modeler will need to select one of the cells in this chart, depending on the characteristics of their model. Application and business represent focus, while relational and dimensional represent functions.

Relational data model

You'll remember from the discussion in Chapter 3 that a relational data model describes the operational databases that support business processes. The scope of a high-level relational data model can range from an individual business process, such as order processing, student registration, or account billing, to an enterprise perspective of all of the concepts encompassed by the business. A sample business rule from a relational model would state, "A Customer must place one or more Orders. An Order must be placed by one and only one Customer."

Dimensional data model

A dimensional model is used exclusively for reporting, as we discussed in Chapter 3. A number such as Gross Sales Amount might need to be viewed at a month or year level, or at a region or country level, for example. The relationships on a high-level dimensional model represent navigation paths between concepts instead of business rules, as in the relational model. For example, a business rule on a dimensional data model would state "I need to see Sales Amount by Customer, Month, and Product. Then I plan on going up to a Year and Brand level."

The scope of a dimensional model is a collection of related measures that together address some business concern. For example, the metrics Number of Product Complaints and Number of Product Inquiries can be used to gauge product satisfaction.

Business perspective

A business perspective is a high-level data model of a defined portion of the business. The scope can be limited to a department or function such as manufacturing or sales or it can be as broad as the entire enterprise or industry. The business perspective is chosen more frequently over the application perspective. Many times when we say we are creating a high-level data model, we mean the business perspective. Before embarking on any large development effort, we first need to understand the business. If an organization needs a new claims-processing system, it needs to have a common understanding of claims and related concepts. The business perspective can be created simply to understand a business area, or as a beginning to a large development effort, such as introducing third-party software into your organization.

Choose the business perspective for any of the following situations:

- **Understanding a business area.** The most popular usage is to gain understanding into an area of the business. It could be the way the business works today or the way the business would like to work at some time in the future. Recall Step 1.
- **Designing an enterprise model.** An enterprise data model must initially be designed at the concept level. Many times we recommend not getting any more detailed than the high-level data model due to the complexities and maintenance issues with hundreds of entities and thousands of data elements.
- **Starting a new development effort.** The business perspective is a very good place to start capturing the concepts and business rules for a new application. All future concept and logical data models can be based on this initial model.

Recently, we built a HDM with a business perspective for a large university. It was built as a prerequisite to building the university's enterprise data warehouse. First business and IT needed to agree collectively on the terms and business rules (i.e. in order to complete this business HDM), and then they could use this model as a scoping tool for deciding on which data mart to build first in their data warehouse.

Application perspective

An application perspective is a high-level data model of a defined portion of a particular application. This perspective can be for either a proposed or existing application. In many cases, the application perspective is built after first understanding the business perspective and is usually a subset of its business perspective. For example, if a business perspective models order processing, the application perspective may focus on an order entry system.

Choose the application perspective for any of the following situations:

- **Understanding an application.** If you need to understand a current or proposed application, the application perspective should be chosen. Recall Step 1. An application might describe concepts using different terminology and enforcing different rules than the actual business area, and therefore this terminology and set of rules needs to be shown on the model.
- **Starting a new development effort.** Ideally, the application perspective HDM should be completed prior to logical design. This way, terminology, rules, and definitions can be agreed upon prior to detailed project analysis. It will save time, money, and unpleasant surprises further down in the software lifecycle.

We once built a HDM with an application perspective to capture the classifications concept in SAP/R3. In an effort to understand how SAP treats classifications (terminology, rules, and definitions), we created this model from studying screens, help files and a large quantity of the underlying 350 database tables. Figure 8.1 contains a subset of this model.

Figure 8.1 – Subset of SAP/R3 Classifications

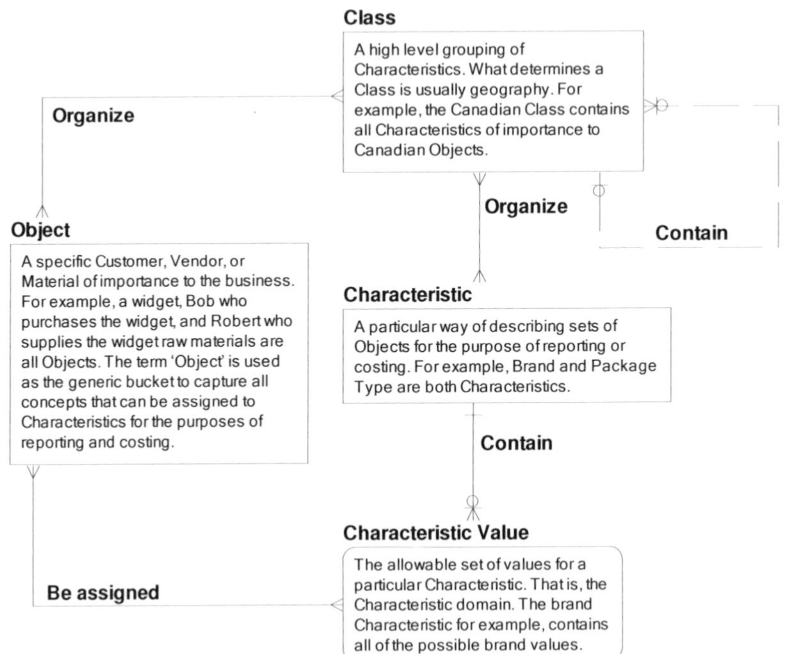

Business rules:

- Each Class may contain one or many Classes.
- Each Class may belong to one Class.
- Each Class must contain many Characteristics.
- Each Characteristic must belong to many Classes.
- Each Characteristic may contain one or many Characteristic Values.
- Each Characteristic Value must belong to one Characteristic.
- Each Class must organize many Objects.
- Each Object must be organized by many Classes.
- Each Object must be assigned many Characteristic Values.
- Each Characteristic Value must be assigned to many Objects.

Note that although the relationships have verb phrases in only one direction, business rules in the other direction can often be articulated using the inverse of the verb phrases that appear.

This SAP/R3 HDM was used for educational purposes as well as to gauge the effort in making customizations to the application. Notice that on this particular model, showing the definitions directly on the model helps the reader to understand the concepts, as terms such as Object and Class can be ambiguous. This model was first used in a joint IT and business department meeting where the goal was to clearly explain SAP/R3 Classifications in 30 minutes or less. This was not an easy task as SAP/R3 is a very complicated system, and showing the audience the underlying 350 database tables with the Classifications area would most likely have led to the audience running screaming from the room. Therefore, this model was produced to get the main concepts across to the audience. Somewhere hidden in those 350 database tables are these four key concepts and accompanying business rules. The model was extremely well-received, and I know from the comments and questions from the audience that both the business and IT folks got it.

STEP 5: SELECT APPROACH

There are three approaches for building a high-level data model: top-down, bottom-up and hybrid. Even though these approaches sound completely different from each other, there is really quite a lot in common across them. In fact, the major difference between the approaches lies in the initial information gathering step.

The top-down approach starts with a purely business need perspective. We learn how the business works and what the business needs from business people, either through direct meetings with the business, or indirectly through requirements documents and reports. The business is allowed to dream and all requirements are considered possible and doable. If a business user discovered an old lamp while looking for shells on the beach, and upon rubbing the lamp a genie appeared and granted the user three wishes, at least one of these wishes should match their ideal set of requirements for an application. This is what we want to capture. The business should aim for the sky.

Ideas are accepted even if we know there is no way to deliver the requirement in today's application environment. For example, imagine if a business user describes their business with the concept of 'Consumer' as the focal point. Although you know today there is very little information being captured on Consumer, it is still important to capture the concept on the HDM because it could be how the business *should* work as opposed to *currently* works today.

The bottom-up approach, on the other hand, temporarily ignores what the business needs and instead focuses on the existing systems environment. We build an initial high-level data model by studying the systems that the business is using today. It can include operational systems that run the day-to-day business or it can include reporting systems that allow the business to view how well the organization is doing. Once the existing systems are understood at a high level, new concepts can be introduced or existing concepts modified to meet the business needs. For example, 'Consumer' may not appear on the initial bottom-up model. After reviewing this model with the business, they might then identify that Consumer is indeed something that should be included.

The hybrid approach is iterative and usually completes the initial information gathering step by starting with some top-down analysis and then some bottom-up analysis, and then some top-down analysis, etc., until the information gathering is complete. First, there is some top-down work to understand project scope and high-level business needs. Then, there is a need to work bottom-up to understand the existing systems. The whole process is a constant loop of reconciling what the business needs with what information is available.

Figure 8.2 summarizes these three information gathering approaches.

Figure 8.2 – Information Gathering Approaches

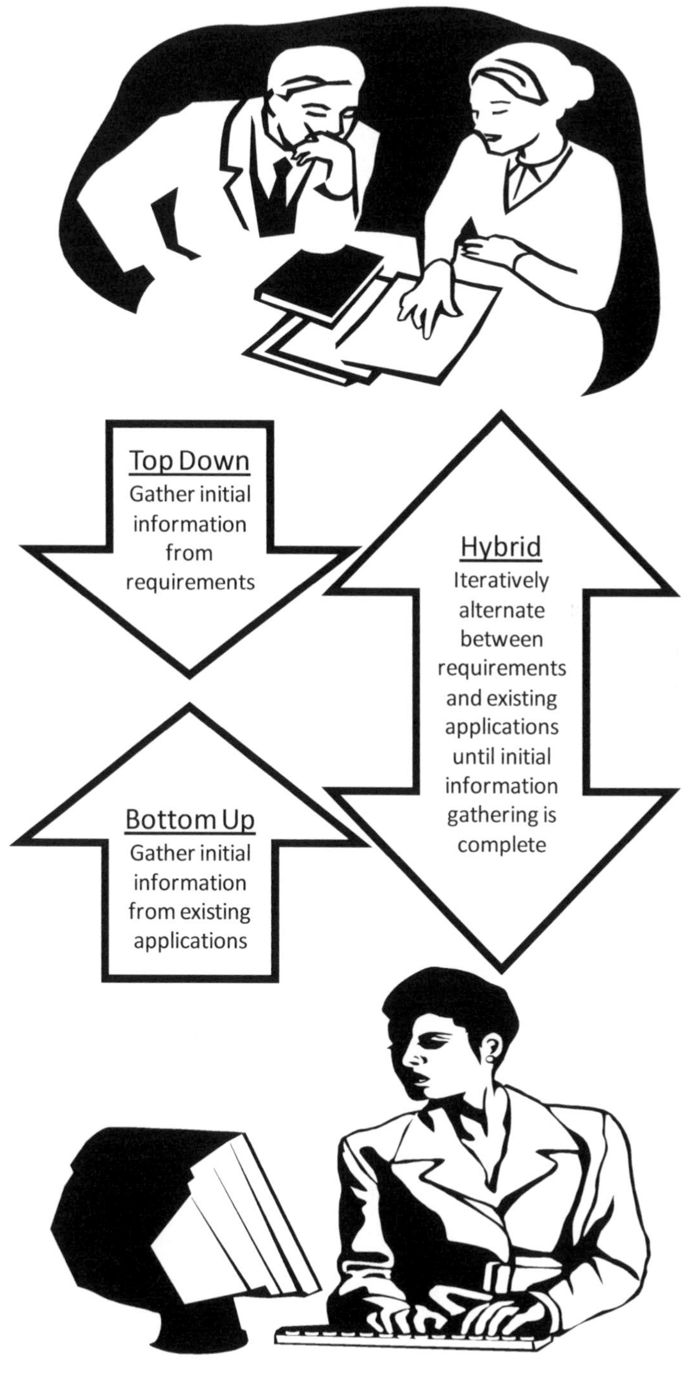

When to choose which approach

If there are minimal business resources available and ample systems documentation, and the purpose of the model is to understand an existing application, a bottom-up approach is ideal. If a new system is being built from scratch and there are business experts eager to participate in the project, a top-down approach would be more appropriate. If a new system is being planned, or an upgrade to an existing system, and business expertise is available and required, a hybrid approach is best. Most high-level models tend to be built using the hybrid approach because there is a need to understand the existing application environment before building something new. Table 8.5 summarizes when to use each approach.

Table 8.5 – When to Use Each Approach

	Capture existing business process	Capture proposed business process	Capture existing application	Capture proposed application
Ample business resources	top-down	top-down	hybrid	top-down
Ample IT resources	hybrid	hybrid	bottom-up	hybrid

When you have both ample business and IT resources available, we would recommend you choose the hybrid approach. It has a nice balance of top-down and bottom-up and therefore chances increase that you'll build the right model.

Example:

Order processing is currently performed with many manual activities. Although eventually there will be an application to automate these activities, your first step is to understand the existing business process. Business resources are anxious to participate.

Because our goal is to capture an existing business process and there are ample business resources available, it makes sense to use the top-down approach. Through meetings with business resources and by extracting concepts out of business and functional requirements documents, one can complete this order processing HDM.

Now You Try It! Selecting the Correct Approach

Decide on which approach you would take for each scenario below, and then turn to the answers in Appendix A to see our solutions with more explanation for each one. Check the most appropriate column for each scenario in Table 8.6.

Table 8.6 – Now You Try It! Selecting the Correct Approach

Scenario	Top-Down	Bottom-Up	Hybrid
Proposed data mart within a current data warehouse architecture. Available business users know exactly what they want.			
Proposed new functionality to an existing operational or data mart application. IT resources are available but little involvement from the business.			
Replacing an existing application. Both business and IT resources are available.			
Customization to packaged software. The business knows what they want and the packaged software documentation is poor. Also there are few technical resources who know the system.			

STEP 6: COMPLETE THE AUDIENCE-VIEW HDM

Once we are confident about which approach we should take, we need to build the audience-view HDM. This is the first high-level model we build. Our purpose is to capture the viewpoint of the audience without complicating information capture with including how their viewpoint fits with other departments or with the organization as a whole. Our next step will reconcile the deliverable from this step with enterprise terminology. Here our purpose is just to capture *their* view of the world.

Top-down

If the approach taken is a top-down approach, initial information gathering in the form of studying requirements documents or interviewing business users is a good starting point. Using the top-down approach, information gathering focuses on what the business wants. The initial model can be created by standing at a whiteboard or flipchart with the users. Sometimes 30 minutes at a whiteboard with a business user can reveal more about what they want than spending hours reading requirements documents. Some teams even make use of note cards and sticky notes that can be pinned to the wall and moved around easily (see Figure 8.3 below). The top-down approach also helps build a strong rapport with the business.

Figure 8.3 – Building a HDM Top-Down as a Group

If a requirements document already exists, the top-down approach can begin by identifying those nouns in the document that are candidates for concepts. For example, in the paragraph of text in Figure 8.4, those in bold and larger font indicate potential concepts for this model.

Figure 8.4 – Sample Text Containing HDM Concepts

This section contains an overview to CII including key concepts, mission statement, business driver and goal. CII is an ***organization*** *that plays the role of intermediary between* ***companies*** *and* ***consumers****. They are the point of contact for the* ***consumer*** *and provide* ***companies*** *with valuable information about their* ***products****. For example, let's say you purchase a* ***product*** *that you are not satisfied with. There happens to be a telephone number on the packaging of the product and you decide to call and voice your* ***complaint****. CII answers these calls for many* ***companies*** *(these* ***companies*** *are CII's* ***customers****), and provides the* ***companies*** *with information so, among other things, they can respond to you with* ***coupons, a phone call, free products****, etc.*

It is often difficult to start from scratch when using the top-down approach. It's a daunting task to stand in front of a completely clean white board or flipchart and ask a room full of people what they need; and it's not always easy for the room full of people to articulate what they want. In these situations, it's a good idea to do some homework and present a starter model that can be torn apart or molded into what the business needs. You can use a model that you began yourself, a high-level industry data model or an XML messaging standard. If you are putting together a starter model for the meeting, it can be as simple as a list of concepts you know will be included, such as Customer and Product. If you are considering using an industry standard such as an industry standard data model or XML messaging standard, stay tuned, we'll talk more about how to leverage industry standards in the next chapter.

A starter model can also be at a higher level than the HDM. Walking into a room with a very high-level data model (VHDM) can be great starting point, as well. For example, recall the paragraph of text from Figure 8.4 where bolded terms included ***coupons, a phone call,*** and ***free products.*** In a VHDM, these concepts might be captured with the more encompassing concept 'Response'. Then in the HDM, Response can be subtyped into Coupon, Phone Call, and Free Product. See Figure 8.5.

Figure 8.5 – Using the VHDM as a Starter Model

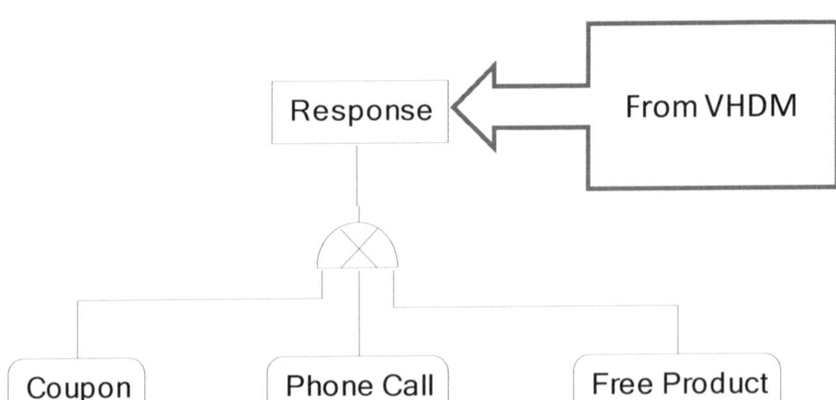

The top-down approach relies heavily on meetings with the users, initially ignoring the existing systems. Eventually we will have to map to the existing systems, but we can do this much later in the requirements process. In the 1980s and early 1990s during the Information Engineering boom, these meetings were called Joint Application Development (JAD) sessions. The term 'JAD' is rarely used anymore, but the same types of meetings take place today under different names, such as 'User Requirements Gathering Sessions'. In these meetings, people who play different roles on the project, from business users to analysts to modelers and developers, work together to document a solution. Let's look at an example based on an actual project that used the top-down approach.

Reinforcing the Top-Down Approach – Recipe Management Audience-View HDM

- Steve's real-world experience

A global manufacturing organization is performing global integration across a number of operational areas. One of these areas is Recipe Management. Recipe Management is responsible for all of the recipes for this global manufacturing company. This includes maintaining the ingredients for each finished product, as well as the quantities of each ingredient and the sequence and timing of each ingredient's entry into the mix. There are many local systems that manage recipes and in many cases the same recipe may be slightly different in different countries. For example, Fuzzy Soda is a popular drink this manufacturing company produces. Figure 8.6 shows the Fuzzy Soda recipes from the US and Spain.

Figure 8.6 – Fuzzy Soda Recipes from the US and Spain

US Recipe for Fuzzy Soda:	**Spain Recipe for Fuzzy Soda:**
List of Ingredients:	List of Ingredients:
2 tablespoons Sugar	2 tablespoons Cane Sugar
1 teaspoon Vanilla	1 teaspoon Vanilla
1/4 teaspoon Chocolate Sprinkles	1/4 teaspoon Mixed Sprinkles
1 teaspoon Lemon Juice	1 teaspoon Lime Juice
1 cup Club Soda	1 cup Sparkling Soda

Both of these recipes are for the same finished product, yet the ingredients are slightly different. For example:

- Is there a difference between 'Sugar' and 'Cane Sugar'?
- Why mixed sprinkles in one recipe and chocolate sprinkles in the other?
- Is there a difference between 'Club Soda' and 'Sparkling Soda'?

Perhaps these recipes are so different that they really produce two distinct products instead of one.

One of the major challenges of building this global recipe system is that different parts of the world may have different definitions for the same terms, the same definitions for different terms, a different sequence of mixing in ingredients, and need different quantities of the same ingredient. In summary, there is no single recipe management view.

Having so many different views of the same concepts, the global project team for Recipe Management decided to build a HDM as one of the first deliverables. They assigned me as the data modeler for this project. I knew right away that if we were ever to complete the project, we would need to take a step back and instead of looking at each country's implementation of Recipe Management, focus on what the new global view should look like. Therefore, I chose the top-down approach for this project. Our goal was to build a better world for Recipe Management. The top-down approach allowed us to take a broader perspective, ignoring the quirks and differences in existing applications and instead focusing on what could be.

The Recipe Management HDM was built completely without face-to-face meetings. To avoid the expense and time of travel, representatives from each country worked at their desks and we communicated via phone and desktop sharing. Video conferencing technology was available, but not ideal because it was easy to talk over one another and the video quality reminded us of something out of a Max Headroom commercial.

CAUTION: International phone calls can be very challenging because you can't see how the person actually feels. For example, you can't see whether the other person has their hands crossed or a stern look on their face. Strong accents and voice tones can also make it difficult to understand and communicate. (You should hear my strong Long Island accent!) I usually do much more listening than talking when on international calls.

With so many representatives globally working on Recipe Management, I decided to meet with small groups of individuals, instead of meeting with everyone in one big virtual meeting. This way everyone could contribute and I could consolidate the outcomes from the smaller group meetings, bringing in larger groups as the project progressed. The larger groups were brought together if there were specific issues that needed to be resolved and at the end of the process when we had one final group review. If, after meeting with individuals from the US and Spain for example, I learned their definition of Recipe was very different than Canada's definition, I would bring representatives from Spain, US, and Canada together in the next round of meetings to resolve this definition issue.

When I first began meeting with the smaller groups, I asked each the same question: "What do you do?" This simple and innocent question can really get the conversation going. It's not about identifying concepts and business rules, but instead about learning how each group works. When the conversation started getting too detailed, I would bring them back up again and move on to the next concept to discuss.

Each of these small group meetings produced an audience model. You can see two different models for the Fuzzy Soda example in Figure 8.7.

Figure 8.7 – Different HDMs in US vs. Spain

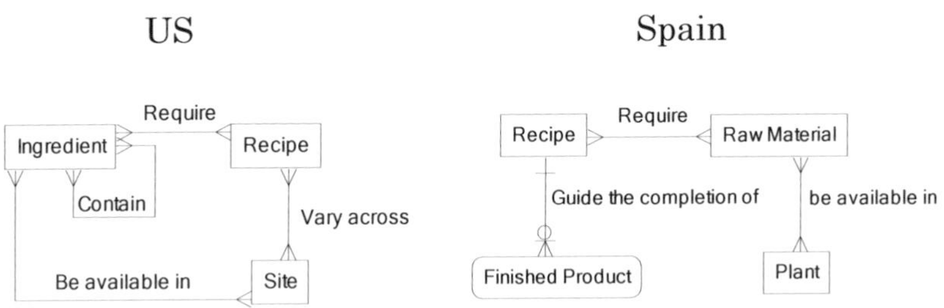

Looking at just two models of the same content, think about some of the questions that will be need to be answered to create a single model of this area. Here are just a few of the many questions:

- How do Site and Plant compare?
- Are Ingredient and Raw Material the same thing?
- Is there a relationship between Raw Materials similar to the relationship between Ingredients in the US?
- How is the concept of Finished Product represented in the US?
- Is Recipe interpreted the same way in the US and Spain?

What other questions would you ask?

Now imagine this effort multiplied by each new recipe model we need to incorporate! That is, what if there were ten models instead of just two?

Bottom-up

The bottom-up approach starts with the existing systems environment. We 'reverse engineer' existing systems, which means we take the actual database design from an existing system and work our way up to the high-level data model. We can create several data models, starting with a physical, then work our way up to a logical, and finally to a high-level data model. We then modify the high-level data model to meet the business' new needs and 'forward engineer' the changes down to the logical and physical models, eventually implementing the new functionality that does what the business needs it to do.

If we are a 'dreamer' with the top-down approach, then we are a 'realist' with the bottom-up approach. We know that eventually the business requirements have to have some relationship with existing applications so why not base the requirements upon the existing systems?

With the bottom-up approach, we perform 'data archeology'[4] by examining sometimes hundreds of pages of documents and thousands of tables, and rolling them up into concepts. Data archeology means we are looking at columns in tables and trying to figure out what their purpose is in life, similar to an archeologist who is trying to piece together shards of clay to determine whether they come from a pot or a vase. For one project I worked on, I scanned over 600 pages of documentation from an ERP system and identified a handful of concepts for the HDM. (- Steve) Let's look at an example based on an actual project using the bottom-up approach.

Reinforcing the Bottom-up Approach – Consumer Interaction Audience-View HDM Example

- Steve's real-world experience

As the data modeler for a large data warehouse, I spent a considerable amount of my time learning how the different

[4] The term 'data archeology' was coined by Dave Wells, Industry Expert

operational systems that feed the data warehouse worked. One of the proposed operational systems was called Consumer Interaction.

Consumer Interaction was the data entry system where users recorded what consumers said via phone and email about the company's products. So, for example, if a consumer bought this company's product in a store and found something wrong with the product, they could call the toll-free number on the product's packaging or send an email to the company. Consumer Interaction was the system where this consumer feedback was recorded.

There was a need to build a reporting system that accepted data from Consumer Interaction and allowed business users to run queries to determine where the most complaints were coming from, for example. All of the information for this new reporting system was to come from the Consumer Interaction data entry system. Therefore, if we could understand this data entry system, we could use it as a scoping tool with the business. We could ask questions to learn more about what the business needed, such as:

- What is a Consumer? That is, can a Consumer be someone who has not yet purchased the product? Another example; what if an attorney calls on behalf of a Consumer who is initiating legal action against the organization for pain suffered by his or her client as a result of something found in a product, would this attorney be considered a Consumer as well? If not, how would this attorney be represented on the data model?
- Can an Interaction be placed by more than one Consumer?
- What types of complaints do you receive?

This system was built using a proprietary database and the application vendor did not give us access to their logical and physical data models. 'Proprietary' is a dirty word within information technology for this very reason—most proprietary systems are 'black boxes' and undocumented, making it difficult to understand them and integrate them with other systems. I therefore needed to create my view of their database at a high-level. A subset is shown in Figure 8.8.

Figure 8.8 – Consumer Interaction Audience-View HDM

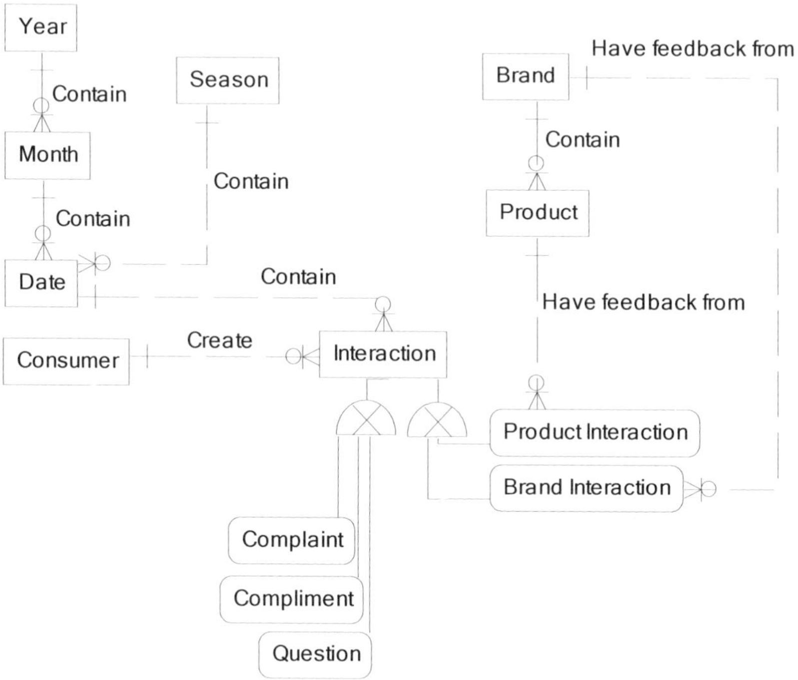

Concept definitions:

Brand – A grouping of products that is recognized by consumers.

Brand Interaction - Connects particular feedback to a specific brand.

Complaint – Negative feedback that we receive on one of our products.

Compliment – Positive feedback that we receive on one of our products.

Consumer - Someone who buys or receives products or services from us with the intent of the products or services being used and not resold; in other words, the final recipient of the product or service. For example, we are a consumer any time we purchase a product from one of our customers.

Date – A period of time containing 24 hours.

Interaction - A contact between an employee and a consumer for a specific product. An interaction can take place through a variety of medium such as through phone, email, and mail. Interactions fit into one of three categories: complaints, compliments and questions. Here are examples of some of the interactions:

- "I love your product." (compliment)
- "I hate your product." (complaint)
- "I found a strange object in your product." (complaint)
- "Where can I buy your product?" (question)
- "I found your product difficult to assemble." (complaint)

Month – One of the twelve major subdivisions of the year.

Product - The products or services that are offered for sale.

Product Interaction – Connects particular feedback to a specific product.

Question – An inquiry that we receive on one of our customer's products.

Season - A season is one of the major divisions of the year, generally based on yearly periodic changes in weather.

Year – A period of time containing 365 days (or 366 days in a leap year).

Business Rules (listed in the order we would typically walk someone through the model):

- Each Year may contain one or many Months. [Note that this is the way the business rule is read based upon the relationship. The data modeling notation we are using is not so precise as to capture a rule such as "Each Year must contain 12 Months."]
- Each Month must belong to one Year.
- Each Month may contain one or many Dates.
- Each Date must belong to one Month.
- Each Season may contain one or many Dates.
- Each Date must belong to one Season.
- Each Brand may contain one or many Products.
- Each Product must belong to one Brand.
- Each Consumer can create one or many Interactions.
- Each Interaction must be created by one Consumer.
- Each Date can contain one or many Interactions.
- Each Interaction must belong to one Date.
- An Interaction can be a Complaint, Compliment, or Question.
- An Interaction can be a Product Interaction or Brand Interaction.
- Each Product can have feedback from one or many Product Interactions.
- Each Product Interaction must be feedback on one Product.
- Each Brand can have feedback from one or many Brand Interactions.
- Each Brand Interaction must be feedback on one Brand.

The purpose of this model was to understand the concepts and high-level business rules within the application that would be brought into a large data warehouse. This model was built bottom-up because I looked at existing extract files to create it and did not base it on user requirements. I performed data archeology on the system, carefully 'picking up' each data element on the extract files and analyzing it to determine what it held and what concept it belonged to.

For example, looking at the C_Last_N data element and seeing values such as 'Jones' and 'Smith', I realized this must be the Consumer Last Name data element and therefore Consumer was the concept that appeared on the model.

This model revealed a very important reporting challenge. One of the reporting requirements was to determine how many interactions are reported at a product brand level. The model shows that interactions can be entered at a product level, which then role up to a brand. Or interactions can come in directly at the brand level. This identifies a very important requirement that IT needs to be aware of. We need to summarize product interactions up to a brand and then add those interactions at just a brand level to get the total number of interactions at a brand level.

Hybrid

If the approach taken is the hybrid approach, we do a bit of both information gathering and data archeology, spending a relatively small amount of time on each and going back and forth between the two techniques until the model is complete. For example, we might spend a few days understanding a subset of the existing application environment, then meet with the business to understand their requirements, which then leads to exploring different parts of the application environment, which leads to more questions on the requirements, and so on until the model is complete. Let's look at an example based on a real project using the hybrid approach.

Reinforcing the Hybrid Approach – Healthcare Audience-View HDM Example

- Steve's real-world experience

I recently worked with a healthcare organization where we used a hybrid approach to build their HDM. Initially, some top-down analysis took place during a meeting with the IT resources. It was also built bottom-up because the IT resources continuously consulted actual systems to learn what concepts they contained, their names for the concepts, and the high-level business rules that constrained the concepts in each system. Very shortly after doing this analysis on the existing systems, meetings were held where we discussed what the business needed. Some concepts created from studying the existing systems were not necessary to capture on the model because they were not part of the requirements. However, other concepts that the business requested did not appear to be present in any of the existing applications. This required more investigation to locate a source for the concepts. These iterations continued until the model was complete. See Figure 8.9.

Figure 8.9 – Healthcare Audience-View HDM

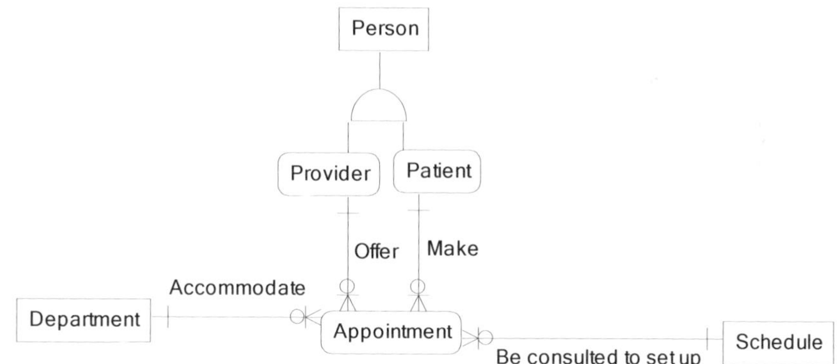

Concept definitions:

Appointment – A scheduled task with an assigned time to be done.

Department – A specialized division of a large organization, such as the Accounting Department.

Patient – A person who requires medical care.

Person – A human being.

Provider – An individual or institution which gives medical care.

Schedule – An ordered list of times at which things are planned to occur.

Business Rules (listed in the order we would typically walk someone through the model):

- A Person can be a Provider, a Patient, or both a Provider and Patient. Note: This is an inclusive (overlapping) subtype, meaning a member of the supertype can play more than one subtype role. For example, a particular person can be both a provider and a patient.
- A Provider can offer one or many Appointments.
- A Patient can make one or many Appointments.
- A Schedule can be consulted to set up one or many Appointments.
- A Department can accommodate one or many Appointments.
- An Appointment must involve one Provider, one Patient, one Department, and one Schedule.

Behind the boxes and lines: definitions, definitions, definitions

For all of these techniques, definitions need to be taken very seriously. Too often we wait until it is too late in the development process to get definitions. Waiting too long usually leads to not writing definitions altogether or doing a rush job in writing quick definition phrases that have little or no usefulness. If the definitions behind the terms on a data model are nonexistent or poor, multiple interpretations become a strong possibility. Imagine a business rule on our model that states that an employee must have at least one benefits package. If the definition of *employee* is lacking, we may wonder, for example, whether this business rule includes job applicants and retired employees.

Definitions agreed-upon at the concept level will make the more detailed logical and physical analysis go smoother and take less time. For example, definitions can address the question, "Does Customer include potential customers or only existing customers?" See the cartoon in Figure 8.10 for an example of what not to do.

Figure 8.10 – Clarify Key Concept Definitions Early!

There are several techniques for writing a good definition. One I like in particular is to write the definition as if you are explaining the term to a child. You wouldn't use many big words or restate the obvious. It also would not be too verbose as a child may not have the same attention span as we do when we get older. Other techniques include avoiding using the name of the term being defined in its definition (e.g. "The Customer

Identifier is the identifier of the customer.") and expanding definitions with examples where appropriate.

There are three main reasons why definitions are important:

- **Assists business and IT with decision making**. If a business user has a different interpretation of a concept than what was actually implemented, it is easy for poor decisions to be made, compromising the entire application. If a business user would like to know how many products have been ordered each month, for example, imagine the poor judgments that could result if the person expected raw materials to be included with products and they were not, or if he or she assumed that raw materials were not included but they were.
- **Helps initiate, document and resolve different perspectives on the same concept**. Folks in accounting and sales can both agree that Customer is an important concept. But can both groups agree on a common definition? If they can agree, you are a step closer to creating a holistic view of the business.
- **Supports data model precision**. A data model is supposed to be precise and unambiguous. An *order line* cannot exist without a *product,* for example. However, if the definition of *product* is missing or vague, we have less confidence in the concept and its relationships. Is a *product,* for example, raw materials and intermediate goods, or only a finished item ready for resale? Can we have an order for a *service,* or must a *product* be a tangible deliverable? The definition is needed to support the *product* concept and its relationship to *order line.*

> ***Tip: Give definitions a priority.*** Everyone can agree that 'Customer' is an important concept, but can you agree on a single definition? Recently, during a presentation to over 100 business analysts, I asked the innocent question, "How many of you have an agreed upon single definition of Customer in your organization?" I was expecting at least a handful of the 100 participants to raise their hands, but no one in the room raised their hand! - Steve

STEP 7: INCORPORATE ENTERPRISE TERMINOLOGY

Once you've captured your stakeholders' view in the boxes and lines of the audience high-level model, you can move on to the enterprise perspective. To build the enterprise perspective, modify the audience model to be consistent with enterprise terminology and rules. Ideally, this enterprise perspective is captured within an enterprise data model.

An enterprise data model is a subject-oriented and integrated data model containing all of the data concepts produced and consumed across an entire organization. Subject-oriented means that the concepts on a data model fit together as the CEO sees the company, as opposed to how individual functional or department heads see their view of the company. There is one Customer concept, one Order concept, etc. Integration goes hand in hand with subject-orientation. Integration means that all of the data and rules in an organization are depicted once and fit together seamlessly. Every data concept has a single definition and name. Integration implies that with this single version of the truth comes a mapping back to the chaotic real world.

An enterprise data model could exist at the VHDM or HDM level, or it could exist at the logical or even possibly the physical level of detail. If the enterprise data model exists at the HDM level, it should still fit on one page, although the paper size might have to be a bit larger ☺. We have built an enterprise HDM that contained over 100 concepts and still fit in a readable font on an 8.5 by 14 inch piece of paper. The comparison between your HDM and the enterprise data model becomes a more tedious task if the enterprise data model exists in a more detailed format, such as logical or physical. For example, there could be over 100 entities that have the word 'Order' in their name on a logical enterprise data model. All of these order entities could map to your HDM concept of 'Purchase Order'.

Most organizations do not have a useable enterprise data model. If you work for one of these organizations, don't worry—there are other ways to ensure an enterprise fit. Other options include matching a system of record, ensuring consistency with a global data warehouse, or comparing your model against an industry standard data model.

You might find yourself renaming concepts or modifying scope to stay in line with the enterprise. More than likely, you will need to go back to the business people for your HDM and confirm both your understanding and theirs of the important concepts on the model. You might have to schedule meetings between the people whose view is captured in the audience-specific model and those who share the enterprise perspective to resolve any terminology or definition issues.

Reinforcing the Top-down Approach – Recipe Management Enterprise-View HDM

- Steve's real-world experience

Returning to the earlier Recipe Management example, if we were able to achieve consensus across all countries, such as the US and Spain, on a single recipe management view, we now need to compare this single audience-view HDM with the enterprise. If we did not achieve consensus across countries, have no fear. We can use the enterprise data model as a medium to bridge concept terminology and definition gaps across the separate HDMs that have been created for each country.

Although this organization did not have a fully-embraced enterprise data model, there were organization-recognized experts. Incorporating these experts' views would guarantee an enterprise view. There were quite a number of passionate conversations and debates at this point to gain alignment between the audience- and enterprise- views.

There was a very important conversation that happened during one of these meetings that is worth summarizing here, although I will change the names of individuals and countries to protect the innocent. Sadie is responsible for Recipe Management in Spain and is one of the primary sources of information for the audience-view HDM. Jamie is the world-renown expert on manufacturing, whose view it is important to match. They are both very well-respected in their departments and each has more than 12 years of experience in their respective fields. The discussion was around Ingredient and Raw Material. Figure 8.11 summarizes a subset of the discussion by phone.

Figure 8.11 – Ingredient vs. Raw Material

Set opens. A phone conference call with Sadie and Jamie. Good mornings and good afternoons follow depending on time zones. I announce that the reason for the call is to resolve definition differences between the terms raw material and ingredient. Sadie starts.

Sadie: I use raw material and ingredient interchangeably. They mean the same thing. Sometimes people prefer the term 'raw material', sometimes 'ingredient' – I use whatever term they are most comfortable with.

Jamie: I have a difference of opinion here. [NOTE: 'Difference of opinion' is a nice way of saying that the other person is wrong.] We define a raw material and ingredient as completely different concepts. A raw material is the most atomic form of input to our recipes, yet an ingredient is not always limited to such an atomic form. Sometimes an ingredient of one product can be the finished goods of another product. For example, in our beverage line, one of the primary raw materials is water. We process the water into distilled water. Distilled water is the primary ingredient for all of our sodas. We also treat this distilled water as a separate finished product when we sell it as bottled water.

Sadie: You are completely wrong - they are the same.

Jamie: Not the same.

Sadie: Same.

Jamie: Not.

```
Five more minutes of explanation, some name calling, virtual fist fighting, and finally resolution:

Sadie: Ok, I understand that they are different. I will not use these terms interchangeably again. I learned something new. Thank you.
```

How the resolution was actually achieved was by walking through in much detail real examples and showing that indeed there was a difference between a raw material and an ingredient. The real conversation that resulted in consensus went more like this:

```
Sadie: You are completely wrong - they are the same.

Jamie: Actually, they are not the same. Let's take an example that you may be able to relate to a bit better. A cocoa leaf would be an ingredient. You'd never use that interchangeably with cocoa powder for making hot chocolate, would you?

Sadie: [Pause] I guess that makes sense. The cocoa leaf would be the raw material, which would be transformed into cocoa powder which is an ingredient in our popular Choco-Latte drink. Huh—I hadn't thought of it that way, because we'd never think of using actual leaves, but your example with the water makes more sense now.

Jamie: Cool. Now let's move on to Recipe.
```

Tip: A few moments of silence are a great facilitation technique. Letting Sadie think about the example gave her time to consider the argument presented and change her way of thinking. No one talking for a few moments might appear awkward, but it can often be the turning point in combative discussions.

There were a number of other conversations like this. At the conclusion of many meetings spanning over two months, we finished our model. A subset is shown in Figure 8.12.

Figure 8.12 – Subset of Ingredient Model

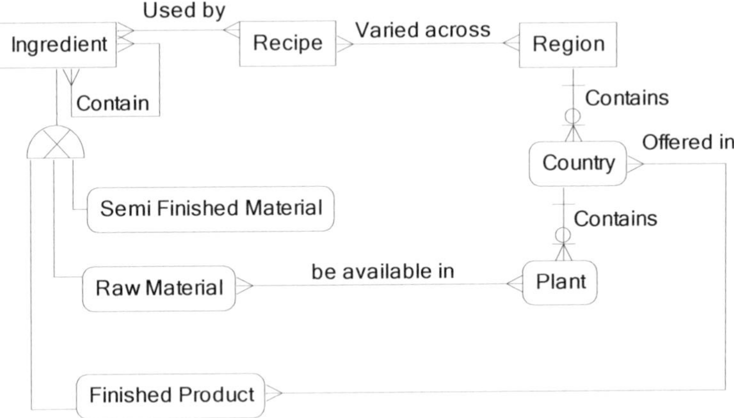

Concept definitions:

Country – A politically organized body of people under a single government.

Finished Product – The final product recognized by the Consumer and in a state ready for sale to our Customers.

Ingredient – Something tangible used in the production process which could be a raw material, the packaging, semi-finished product, or the finished product ready for sale to the consumer.

Plant – The building or buildings, or parts thereof, used for or in connection with the manufacturing, processing, packaging, labeling, or storage of our ingredients.

Raw Material - An unprocessed natural resource or product used in manufacturing.

Recipe - A set of instructions for how to make a finished item ready for sale to the consumer.

Region – A geographic term used to describe one or more countries.

Semi-Finished Material – An ingredient that contains one or more raw materials that have been modified according to a recipe with a goal of being transformed into a finished product.

Business Rules (listed in the order we would typically walk someone through the model):

- An Ingredient must contain many Ingredients.
- An Ingredient must be part of many Ingredients.
- An Ingredient can be a Semi-Finished Material, Raw Material, or Finished Product.
- An Ingredient must be used by many Recipes.
- A Recipe must include many Ingredients.
- Each Recipe must vary across many Regions.
- Each Region must use many Recipes.
- Each Region may contain one or many Countries.
- Each Country must belong to one Region.
- Each Country may contain one or many Plants.
- Each Plant must belong to one Country.
- Each Country must offer many Finished Products.
- Each Finished Product must be offered in many Countries.
- Each Plant must contain many Raw Materials.
- Each Raw Material must be available in many Plants.

STEP 8: SIGNOFF

After the initial information gathering, make sure the model is reviewed for data modeling best practices as well as the fact that it meets the requirements. The sign-off process on a HDM does not require the same formality as signoff on a physical design, but it should still be taken seriously. Usually email verification that the model looks accurate will suffice.

Validating whether or not the model has met data modeling best practices is often done by applying the Data Model Scorecard®. The Data Model Scorecard® contains 10 categories for validating a data model. Table 8.7 shows the Scorecard template and a short summary of each category follows.

Table 8.7 – Using the Data Model Scorecard® for a HDM

#	Category	Total score	Model score	%
1	How well do the characteristics of the model support the type of model?	10		
2	How well does the model capture the requirements?	15		
3	How complete is the model?	15		
4	How structurally sound is the model?	15		
5	How well does the model leverage generic structures?	10		
6	How well does the model follow naming standards?	5		
7	How well has the model been arranged for readability?	5		
8	How good are the definitions?	10		
9	How consistent is the model with the enterprise?	5		
10	How well does the metadata match the data?	10		
	TOTAL SCORE	**100**		

Here is a brief description of each of these ten categories:

1. **Model type**. This question ensures that the high-level model being reviewed meets the definition for a high-level model. Concepts need to be intuitive to a business user with clear definitions. The model should fit neatly on one page. When we see a HDM that is fully attributed and a few steps away from actual database tables, it loses points in this category.
2. **Correctness**. We need to understand the content of what is being modeled. This can be the most difficult of all 10 categories to grade because we really need to understand how the business works and what the business wants from their application. If we are modeling a *sales data mart*, for example, we need to understand the key concepts necessary for sales reporting, including both measures and the levels of detail these measures need to be understood by, such as by Month, Region, and Brand.
3. **Completeness**. This category checks for data model components that are not in the requirements or requirements that are not represented on the model. If the scope of the model is greater than the requirements, we have a situation known as 'scope creep.' If the model scope is less than the requirements, we will be leaving information out of the resulting application, usually leading to an enhancement or 'Phase 2' shortly after the application is in production. For completeness, we need to make sure the scope of the project and model match, as well as ensuring all the necessary metadata on the model is populated. Regarding metadata, there are certain types that tend to get overlooked when modeling, such as definitions and stewardship. A HDM missing key concepts or definitions will lose points in this category.

4. **Structure**. This is the 'Data Modeling 101' category. This category validates the design practices employed to build the model. As we've stressed before, this book is focused on VHDMs and HDMs, so the model structure can take any form and checking it isn't important. But it would become very important if logical and physical models were to be developed from the HDM.
5. **Abstraction**. This category gauges the use of generic concept and relationship structures. One of the most powerful tools a data modeler has at their disposal is abstraction; the ability to increase the types of information a design can accommodate using generic concepts. Going from Customer Location to a more generic Location, for example, allows the design to more easily handle other types of locations, such as warehouses and distribution centers.
6. **Standards**. Correct and consistent naming standards are extremely helpful for knowledge transfer and integration. New team members who are familiar with similar naming conventions on other projects will not lose time learning a new set of naming standards. This category focuses on naming standard structure, abbreviations, and syntax. In reviewing a HDM, we would expect all concept names to be singular, they should represent information instead of processes, and relationship names should be verbs, for example.

7. **Readability**. This question checks to make sure the model is visually easy to follow. Readability needs to be considered at a model, concept, and relationship level. At a model level, we like to see a large model broken into smaller logical pieces. At the concept level, one popular technique is to place child concepts below parent concepts. Child concepts are on the many side of the relationship and parent concepts are on the one side of the relationship. So if an Order contains many Order Lines, Order Line should appear below Order. At a relationship level, we try to minimize relationship line length, the number of direction changes a relationship line makes and the number of relationships crossing each other. We also look for missing or incomplete relationship labels. Refer to Chapter 4 for more on enhancing model readability.
8. **Definitions**. This category includes checking all definitions to make sure they are clear, complete, and correct. Clarity means that a reader can understand the meaning of a term by reading the definition only once. Completeness ensures the definition is at the appropriate level of detail and that it includes all the necessary components, such as derivations and examples. Correctness focuses on having a definition that totally matches what the term means and is consistent with the rest of the business.
9. **Consistency**. Does this model complement the 'big picture'? The structures that appear in a data model should be consistent in terminology and usage to structures that appear in related data models and with the enterprise model, if one exists. This way there will be consistency across projects. If a Marketing HDM contains the term 'Customer' and the enterprise HDM calls this concept a 'Prospect', we would need to resolve this difference.

10. **Data**. This category determines how well the concepts and their rules match reality. Collecting real data can be difficult to do early in a project's lifecycle, but the earlier, the better so you can avoid future surprises that may be much more costly. If data surprises are not caught during the design phase, they will probably be caught during system testing or user acceptance testing at a much higher cost of time and money. A quick look at the data for the Customer concept, for example, can reveal whether Customer is always a company or can also be an individual.

Once the model is complete, you will need signoff from the model's audience, most likely a business user or business manager. If the audience member or members responsible for signing off on the model have been involved in building the model, the signoff should just be a formality. Having signoff is critical to the credibility of the model.

STEP 9: MARKET

Think of yourself as a product vendor of sorts—the best product on the market won't necessarily sell unless it is marketed effectively. And the best-advertised product won't sell unless it solves a need of the consumer. Marketing is about understanding the customer's motivations (i.e. what's in it for me?), creating a plan to accomplish a win – win scenario, and then making sure to get the word out to the appropriate audience.

In building a successful high-level modeling project, it is important to treat the marketing aspect as a project in and of itself. To that end, make sure to create a specific communication plan as part of your project's deliverables. This communication plan outlines both the message and the target community.

The development of a marketing plan includes the following process steps

1. Identify the target audience / customer
2. Identify the pain point(s) and desired result
3. Develop a customer motivation profile
4. Identify marketing resource constraints
5. Develop the message
6. Identify the media channel
7. Develop a communication plan

1. Identify the target audience / customer

We've already defined our stakeholders in building the model in Step 2. In this step, we're looking at these same individuals as our potential customers, rather than as the members of the team building the model. It's now time to 'sell' them on the idea of how successful this model is and how it will help them in their daily jobs, make more money for the company, etc. Since we already thought of this in Step 1, it shouldn't be new to them, but formalizing the identification of the stakeholders for your marketing plan is a helpful way of making sure that once the model is complete, you're going back to the right people to let them know what a great thing it is.

2. Identify the pain point and desired result

In marketing the model, it's important to go back to the purpose we defined in Step 1. What pain did we solve with this model? How does it help people improve a specific process in the organization? How does it help the organization, in general? With an HDM, your reasons will probably include a reference to alignment among different areas of the organization on terminology and rules, the ability to share data for corporate-wide initiatives and possibly opportunities to improve data cleanliness.

It's also important to identify the desired result of this marketing effort. If we're selling soap, the answer is easy—we want consumers to buy more soap. But with a data model, the desired actions are more diverse. For example, you might decide that you want the data quality program to utilize your data modeling environment for all of their new initiatives, or the business sponsor to give you more funding for the next project. For each audience, you need to not only show how the model helps them, but also make sure to let them know what you'd like them to do about it.

For example, you might approach the data quality group and say something like "Now that our new Customer HDM has made it easier to see a unified corporate view of customer information, can you make sure that all new initiatives use customer concepts that match this model?" Or you may approach your business sponsor and say "You've seen that your initial investment in consolidating customer information has saved the company $100,000. Would you be willing to make a similar investment for product information to help our new sales campaigns?" It's important to remember to both state the achievements of your group, and let the stakeholders know what you'd like them to do as a next step.

3. Develop a customer motivation profile

Once you have the customers/stakeholders identified, you need to analyze and record the customers' motivations. This will help you fine tune your marketing approach. Put another way, this is the "What's in it for me?" aspect of marketing.

The motivation profile is a list of potential benefits that your target customer could expect to realize if they bought the product advertised in the marketing campaign. For example, if the customer was a data quality program, some of the potential benefits from using a data modeling deliverable would be time saved and better communication with stewards. For each targeted customer, record the customer name and the potential motivator. See Table 8.8 for an example.

Table 8.8 – Sample Customer Motivation Profile

Customer Name	Motivator
Data Quality Program	Completing project on time Engaging with the data stewards Gaining approval from the data owners

4. Identify marketing resource constraints

Every marketing campaign has a resource constraint which may be related to deadlines, budgets, specialized communication, and graphic support. Most likely, your data modeling funding didn't include any extra resources for 'marketing', so you will have to be creative. Understand what your resource constraints are and design your marketing plan around your constraints.

5. Develop the message

Consider what message you wish to communicate. This should be something simple, easy to remember, and memorable. A short four to six word phrase would be ideal. Once you have your phrase, use it in every communication message that you deliver. The key is a simple, consistent message. If you are having difficulty thinking of a message, watch TV for an hour and write down every advertising phrase. These are examples of what you need to develop for your message.

6. Identify the media channel

In the world of advertising, the media channel is the method by which the message gets delivered. Every organization has a media channel. They may be internal publications such as magazines, online portals, and daily reports. Also don't forget to consider free resources or underutilized resources like newsletters and lunch-and-learn forums. For example, many organizations have a monthly newsletter. Editors of these internal newsletters are always looking for interesting stories, announcements, and success stories.

Once the model is complete, word has to get out that it is available for use. If the model has a relatively small scope, it is possible that the users who helped you build and validate the model are also the only ones who need to know about it, so marketing requires little effort. However, most HDMs span broad areas; it is essential to let the appropriate business and IT resources know it is available for use.

There are a number of ways to market the model:

- **Give away free food!** Somehow, the idea of free lunch always packs a room. 'Lunch-and-learns' are a great technique—during a lunch hour anyone can come in to listen to a topic and get free lunch at the same time. It's amazing what a dozen pizza pies can do to promote your product!
- **Make it social!** Why not combine free food with a social event and have an 'ice cream social'? (Have you gotten the idea by now that we like ice cream? ☺) To incent people to join your meeting, send out meeting invites that mention ice cream sundaes, complete with all the toppings. Notice how the wording of the announcement went from data model review, to social? This kicks in the fun factor. While the meeting is in progress, take a photo of the event. After the event, publish a success story, complete with a photo of the event, in one of the community newsletters that the audience receives. Focus on the fun factor, but don't forget to mention the meeting purpose and the benefits, risk, and time savings created by the HDM.

- **Use the Web - 'Advertise' on the Corporate Intranet Site.** Find a web page that receives lots of hits from employees and use it to announce that the model is available and what it will achieve within the business. Publish the HDM itself in HTML format so that business users can take a look. Remember, you might want to call it something other than a 'data model' or 'HDM', if business users aren't used to or dislike that term. Use, for example, a 'business picture' or 'business overview'.
- **Present at a Management Meeting.** This could be a great way for the modeler to get some career visibility with management, as well as tout the model. Remember to focus on the ***business benefits*** you identified in Step 1.
- **Reward Reuse:** Integrate model linkage within the data modeling environment process and reward people who reuse data model objects. On one project, we were even able to get 'object reuse' on developers' career incentive plan to reward them for being a good 'data citizen'.
- **Organize a 'Modeling Overview Tour'** that consists of a series of in-person meetings or webcasts to communicate with stakeholders in all geographic locations. In a multicultural, worldwide organization, be considerate of time zones. The folks in Europe will be more attentive during the morning hours and will appreciate the extra effort that you put into scheduling a meeting during their work day. For each group, make sure to focus on the particular benefits you have identified for them in Step 2 of your marketing plan.
- **Give Away Free Stuff!** Food is not the only incentive to spice up a meeting. You can use books as random drawings to all meeting attendees—technical folks particularly like books as giveaways. (We think buying a copy of this book as a giveaway for each member of your team is a great idea. ☺) For a change of pace, keep

a toy box or a box of candy handy for meetings. For long meetings where attention has waned, giving away an incentive for a good answer to a question often motivates even senior-level executives. It's amazing to continually discover that we're all kids at heart.

- **Distribute a Poster of your Model:** Posters are another favorite, especially among IT workers. Some database companies have created almost a cult following around posters showing their data dictionary (we're not kidding!). In many office complexes, the walls are bare and having something clever and colorful to cover them is always appreciated.
- **Be Part of Company Team-Building or Offsite Events:** If your company hosts annual planning meetings or offsites, volunteer to host a team building event. Don't waste the event on a trust building exercise, use something relevant to data modeling. The key is to make it different, interesting and relevant. If you're successful, the team building participants will learn something new about data modeling. Don't underestimate the ability of non-technical team members to understand a high-level data model. At one sales training event, we had sales representatives build data models around their favorite alcoholic beverages (remember the step of identifying the right motivation for the customer?).

In summary, marketing should be fun. It does not need to cost a lot of money or require assistance from a marketing department (although money and professional communication staff support can be invaluable). Take into account details like cultural differences. Create a timely, relevant, interesting message. Anyone can apply these techniques in their office environment. Volunteer to lead a team building event and make it fun!

"Going Country" With Data Management

- Mona's real-world example

In one campaign, I wanted to communicate that the data modeling environment was part of the larger Data Management Body of Knowledge (DMBOK). The DMBOK functional areas are generally shown in a wagon wheel, with the disciplines divided up by wagon wheel spokes. Using this simple wagon wheel concept, a team building exercise was developed.

The team building exercise was to construct a wagon, pulled by horses. The wagon had to be labeled with the correct Body of Knowledge labels, it had to have at least 2 wheels and it had to be pulled by a horse. The team was given supplies, which consisted of pipe cleaners to build the horses, box candies for the covered wagon, popsicle sticks, feathers, beads, marking pens, construction paper, tape, glue and scissors. The exercise took 90 minutes to complete and at the end of the 90 minutes the participants had constructed a covered wagon, correctly labeled with body of knowledge titles. For this exercise I provided a short 20 minute presentation describing the theory and outlined the team-building rules.

To keep the meeting moving, I played a You Tube clip of a bareback barrel play day that was synchronized to county music. At the end of the 90 minutes the comments that I received ranged to from "Wow!" to "I will never forget this session." Gosh, that's the point!

7. Develop a communication plan

The communication plan is the formal documentation of all of the elements listed above, along with the detailed steps and schedule for delivering the message. As we mentioned, the marketing aspect should be considered a project in and of itself, and formal documentation will not only assist in making sure that this effort goes smoothly, but that you'll have a good reference to get ideas from for your next project.

STEP 10: MAINTAIN

Remember that even after the model is complete, there is still a maintenance task that we must stay on top of. The HDM will not change often, but it *will* change. We need to have formal processes for keeping the model up-to-date and aligned with the other model levels. We also want to make sure that the HDM is actively used by other groups and processes in the organization and doesn't become a passive artifact.

What works well is to have two additional steps in any software methodology:

1. Borrowing from a HDM, and

2. Contributing back to the HDM.

The first step takes place after the HDM is complete. For example, before starting a logical data model, one will need to reference the HDM and most likely use the HDM as a starting point for the logical. The second step in the methodology requires taking all of the learnings that came out of the project, and making sure any new concepts make their way back into the HDM. For example, during the logical data modeling stage the modeler learns that the many-to-many relationship between Student and Course contains the Registration concept. Therefore, Registration might become a new concept on the HDM. The presentation medium of a spreadsheet is a common way of capturing the mapping between a HDM and its related, more detailed logical and physical levels. Most modeling tools support a capability that captures the mapping and allows export into a spreadsheet format for easy viewing. The case study in Chapter 14 contains several examples showing links between different data models.

As with the other steps in building the HDM, it's helpful to have a framework or methodology around the actions needed for the maintenance and publication of the model. We'll describe the basic maintenance steps in Table 8.9. Before that, however, let's describe some of the functions involved.

The Modeling Function. The primary purpose of this function is to create and maintain the data model. This is the function that data management professionals get mostly right—data modelers generally know how to get the graphical representation correct. While the picture is important as a communication tool, the richness of the model is in the underlying metadata that the function is also responsible for gathering. Managing metadata tends to be challenging, but there are robust tool sets that help with data modeling and metadata management.

> I can still remember my first view of a modeling tool. A group of ten of us watched as Carolyn, the repository manager, demonstrated the tool. Sadly, the tool was so centralized that no one really got to touch it. The metadata entered was too difficult for regular folks to touch. Fortunately, modern tools have richer functionality than yesterday's tools, and most tools today can easily generate user-friendly reports and export into HTML or spreadsheet format. - Mona

The Architecture Function. The architecture function is responsible for data architecture integration and ensuring that the high-level data model represents the very high-level view point. The architect ensures that the HDM balances the needs of the ownership and modeling functions while still maintaining a corporate perspective.

The Ownership Function. The ownership function is responsible for reviewing and approving changes. The challenge with this function is ensuring that it is established successfully. Depending upon organizational maturity, the ownership function could consist of a data governance board, a stewardship community, a data ownership forum, or just a single business analyst or sponsor who needs to approve information. The name of the function is not the critical success factor. What is important is that the ownership community assumes responsibility for the planning and control of the data assets by using the high-level data model.

The Data Model Maintenance Processes

Now that we've defined the roles in this process, we'll walk through the various steps of the process, which are outlined in Table 8.9.

Table 8.9 – The High-Level Data Model Maintenance Process

Process Step Number	Process Name	Function Responsible
I	Change Model	Modeling
II	Review Change Request	Architecture
III	Facilitate Peer Review	Architecture
IV	Approve Change	Ownership
V	Implement Change	Modeling
VI	Publish Model	Modeling

I. Change Model

The event that prompts this process is a change in the HDM. This could be a change in a business definition, a change in the name of a concept, an addition or deletion of a concept to or from the model, etc. Model revisions can be grouped into four categories:

A) Changes to the graphical model

B) Changes to the metadata

C) Changes to aesthetic layout

D) Changes in content resulting from project activity

Based on the type of model changes above, the type of maintenance can be classified into the same categories A, B, C, and D. This classification can aid in setting priorities as well, indicating if a heavy or a light touch change management process should be followed. Changes that do not have much impact to the metadata can follow a lightweight process. Changes that have significant metadata will need to follow a more rigorous process. From a communication perspective, the visual appearance of the graphic model is important; however from a change management perspective, it's the metadata management that is significant, not the graphical aspects.

II: Review Change Request

The architecture function is responsible for data architecture integration and ensuring that the high-level data model represents a high enough view point. The purpose of this process step is to review the model to ensure that it represents the high-level view. If new concepts or concept enhancements have been added to the model, then the data architect will need to ensure that the data governance and data ownership functions accept these changes. Each new concept will need to be mapped to a data owner. The data modeler or business user can propose a new concept, but it is the responsibility of the data architect to identify candidate data stewards and/or a data owner to accept the ownership responsibilities of the concept.

Once the revision changes have been accepted, the data architecture function must perform an impact analysis of the change request to determine whether the change will have an adverse affect on any other group or application. In some cases, this might prompt a facilitated discussion between groups about how they might name or define a particular concept.

III: Facilitate Peer Review

We'll go into more detail regarding the Facilitate Peer Review process step in our Ice example. This is often the most challenging aspect of change management, as the 'softer' skills of listening and facilitation are more important to success than technical skills. The goal of this step is to achieve consensus on definitions, terminology, and rules.

IV: Approve Change

Once agreement has been reached, the data owner or steward should have final say in whether this change is accepted. Normally, this is a business person who can give a 'reality check' that this definition, terminology, or rule correctly applies to the business.

V: Implement Change

After the change has been approved, the modeling team actually implements this change in the production version of the HDM, making sure that the change is correctly checked-in through the change management system.

VI: Publish Model

The publication of the model may be one of the most important steps in this maintenance process. If stakeholders are not aware that the change has been made, or that there are new definitions to use, they are not likely to use them, which will exacerbate the 'silos' of information and lack of sharing and reuse.

Case Study: Technology Company

This was a bleeding edge technology company with a heavily customized ERP system geographically located in a Silicon Valley-type community. It was a fast-paced development shop that used a hybrid rapid prototype within a standard ERP blended traditional software development lifecycle (SDLC) environment. The company maintained a staff ratio of 60% employees, 20% consultants and 20% contractors. Most of the consultants were ERP specialists. The information technology community had a mature process infrastructure with governance boards, change management boards, quality management and architecture in place. Their SDLC process included approval to precede steps with architecture reviews and a minimum requirement for data modeling deliverables. All changes to the ERP system required a peer review of the project data models and the associated metadata.

The high-level data modeling publication process consisted of a multiple-focus approach:

- A title block was added to the data model stored in the repository that included the project information, stakeholder information, and approval status.
- A wall chart was printed on a color plotter and delivered to key stakeholders. These wall charts were popular with both the business analysts and developers.
- The internal website was updated with a Word document (embedded graphics) and meaningful metadata. Care was taken to ensure that the reports were easy to read and fit on standard-sized paper. All models included clear English word annotation (i.e. structured English or assertions).
- An email message was sent to a distribution list notifying the community that a new high-level data model had been published. The email included hyperlinks to the web site, and site locations where the wall charts were hung.

Key Points

- There are ten steps required to complete the HDM
- Communication is the main reason behind building a HDM—communicating existing or proposed business or application terminology and rules
- Stakeholders are business and IT professionals who build and/or use the HDM. Participation from both business and IT are required for success
- A HDM can be either relational and capture how the business works, or dimensional and capture how the business is monitored
- There are three approaches for building the high-level data model: top-down, bottom-up and a hybrid of the two
- The audience-view HDM captures the viewpoint of the modeling participants without taking into account how their perspective fits with other departments or with the organization as a whole
- To build the enterprise perspective, modify the audience model to be consistent with enterprise terminology and rules
- Agreed-upon definitions at the concept level will make the more detailed logical and physical analysis go smoother and take less time
- The Data Model Scorecard® is a tool for validating data model quality
- There is a seven-step approach to marketing the HDM
- There is a six-step approach to maintaining the HDM

CHAPTER 9
High-Level Data Model Templates

In addition to traditional data modeling products, there are other helpful tools that make the process of building a HDM more efficient and accurate. These tools are the focus of this chapter. You don't need to use every tool—pick and choose the ones that make sense for your environment and the people you're working with.

In-The-Know Template

The In-The-Know Template captures the people and documentation that can provide and validate the data requirements. It is the result of recording people's names and roles for many projects, and standardizing on a format to capture the most important types of information about each of the project resources. It also includes where other important resources are located. For example, the location of useful documentation for completing data modeling deliverables, such as business and functional requirements documents, is identified. Relying on memory instead of writing the locations down can lead to forgetting how to find the documents. Here is a sample of the types of information captured in this tool:

- Tom Jones has been assigned to your project as the Subject Matter Expert on customer account information. His title is Customer Account Divisional Vice President and he can be reached at...
- The Customer Classification List will help us validate our customer classification data and it can be found on our public drive in the customer folder. It is updated twice a year by the...
- The Current Item Report is run quarterly by the Reference Data Team and we can find the latest copy of this report on their web site at www...

Table 9.1 contains a sample In-The-Know Template.

Table 9.1 – Sample In-The-Know Template

Concept	Resource	Type	Role/ How used	Location /Contact
Customer	Tom Jones	Subject Matter Expert	Customer Reference Data Administrator	212-555-1212
	Customer classification list	Reference document	To validate and create new customer classifications	S:/customer/custclsfn.xls
Item	Current Item Report	Report	To identify all current item information	www.item.com

Here is a description on how each of these columns is used:

- **Concept.** This is the concept name. You can take the list of concepts from the Concept List (the next technique below) and put them right into this column.
- **Resource.** This is the source of the information. In this template, it is broad enough to be anything useful. It includes people, requirement documents, reports, etc. Be as specific as possible in this description column. If there is more than one resource for the same concept, use a separate row in the template for the additional resources. Examples of resources include:

  - Bob Jones
  - Most current customer classification rollups
  - Profitability report for April
  - Reference data department
  - Logistics data mart business requirements document

- **Type.** Provides a general category for each of the resources. Because this template can be so generic, it is important to put each of the resources into the most appropriate category. So, for example, the categories for the above- mentioned resources are put in square brackets:

  - Bob Jones [Subject Matter Expert]
  - Most current customer classification rollups [Report]
  - Profitability report for April [Report]
  - Reference data department [Organization]
  - Logistics data mart business requirements document [Requirements Document]

You can customize the types for your own organization, but this is the level that I've found most useful.

- **Role / How used.** This provides why the resource is valuable to this project. Why are we bothering to list this resource in this template? Be specific! So, for example, the roles for the above- mentioned resources are put in square brackets:

- Bob Jones [XYZ Source system expert]
- Most current customer classification rollups [Report used to make sure customer reference data hierarchy is correct]
- Profitability report for April [Existing report that the users want to expand]
- Reference data department [Area that will need to validate all reference data definitions and names]
- Logistics data mart business requirements document [Most current business requirements document for the new application]

* **Location / Contact.** This column contains how to reach the resource. If the resource is a document, this column might contain the document's path name on the public drive or where to find it on the Web. If the resource is a person, this column might contain the person's phone number, email address, or mailing address. So for the same examples, the location appears within the square brackets:
    - Bob Jones [555-1212]
    - Most current Customer Classification Rollups [www.customergroupetc.com]
    - Profitability report for April [Reporting universe in this folder....]
    - Reference data department [4th floor of building B, manager is James Smith, phone number 555-1212]
    - Logistics data mart business requirements document [ftp this document off of this file server...]

The In-The-Know Template captures the people and documentation that can provide and validate the data requirements. Having this information in a standard format accomplishes several goals:

- **Provides a handy and complete reference list.** This template is easy to read and provides all of the types of information that are necessary to identify people and documentation resources. Even years after the project is in production, this list could still be useful for functional or technical project questions.
- **Finds gaps or redundancy in your available list of resources.** This document will highlight any missing information. For example, if there is no available expert on item information, it will be very evident here. If you are missing a key reference document, you will notice it here and can raise it to management's attention.
- **Acts as a sign off document.** For example, if a person is identified as a resource for a particular concept, their management can be made aware of this and allocate their time accordingly. This way you will minimize the chances that your customer expert is pulled in another direction when you need their help.

Concept List

The Concept List is a handy starting point if you feel it might be too much of a jump to start capturing business rules—that is, the relationships on a data model. The Concept List is a listing of the concepts the business feels are important to capture, without worrying about the terminology on a data model. As your HDM develops, you might need to refine terms and definitions on the Concept List to keep them up-to-date and valuable.

Table 9.2 shows a sample Concept List.

Table 9.2 – Sample Concept List

Name	Synonyms	Definition	Questions
Asset	Machine, Part, Capital, Stock, Wealth, Supplies	Something our company owns that is considered to be valuable.	Does this also include purchases we plan on making for the upcoming year?
Carrier	Trucking Company, Distributor, Transporter	A company that physically moves our products from one site to another site.	Does carrier include both company-owned carriers and externally-owned? Or just our own carriers?
Company	Corporation, Firm, Organization, Partnership	A business enterprise that serves a purpose to society and the economy.	Are our business units or subsidiaries considered separate companies, within a larger company, or do we just have one company?
Contract	Order, Promotion, Agreement, Invoice, Bill of Lading, Bill of Materials, Purchase Order, Policy, Statement	A document containing the terms and conditions around the purchase or creation of product.	What is the difference between a transaction and a contract? Which happens first?

Here is a description of each of the columns:

- **Name**. Name contains the most common name for each concept. Concepts are listed alphabetically by concept name.
- **Synonyms**. This is a great place to list aliases for this term. Often when there is more than one name for the same concept, listing all of the names under Synonyms is a step towards a single name and definition. This column also includes those words that are more specific to a particular industry, or those terms that are a more detailed concept than the concept term. For example, Order in this column is a more specific term for the Contract concept.
- **Definition**. Definition contains a brief description for each of the concepts. The basic definition is designed to be generic enough to be easily customizable, yet detailed enough to provide value.
- **Questions**. Questions contain some questions or comments that might be worthwhile addressing when refining your concept definitions. This last column can be a great conversation starter as well, as these questions can spark lively discussion and debate. Your goal for these questions is to more clearly articulate the definition of a concept by answering what that concept includes or does not include.

The Concept List is a very simple tool which accomplishes a number of important goals:

- **Creates a high-level understanding of the application's concepts.** After completing this checklist, you and the rest of the project team will clearly understand each concept and know what is within the scope of the application. When you start modeling the VHDM or HDM, you will already know the concepts and only have to add the relationships between these concepts to complete the model.

- **Gets your project team 'out from the weeds'.** This is useful when your project team wants to start off the modeling phase by diving directly into the data elements. In these situations, it can be very easy to miss key concepts and therefore accidentally leave out required information. Starting the application analysis by listing data elements creates a narrow and incomplete view of the project's requirements. In order to step back and really understand the scope of the application, you need to have your team view it from a concept level. Taking this view allows people to see a more complete, bigger picture.
- **Facilitates concept and data element names and definitions.** Having solid names and definitions at the concept level makes it easier to develop names and definitions at the more detailed levels. If we have a standard name and very good definition for Customer, for example, than we can more easily name and define the concepts Customer Location and Customer Association, and the data elements Customer Last Name and Customer Type Code.
- **Initiates rapport with the project team and business users.** Completing the Concept List as a group is a very good first data modeling task for you and the rest of the team. It is a quick win, meaning it is not usually very difficult to complete, yet has big payoffs. It can help with understanding the new application's content at a high-level, as well as help build rapport with the project team.

Concept Family Tree

The Concept Family Tree is a spreadsheet that captures the source applications and other key metadata for each concept within the scope of our application. It becomes a necessity when there is more than one source application and sourcing complexities are possible. If your HDM focuses on purely a business perspective (and not an application perspective), the

Concept Family Tree is not necessary. The Concept Family Tree works especially well when our application is a data mart, because this tool can capture which information currently exists in the data warehouse and which applications we will require new information from.

Keeping the sourcing information neatly organized within a spreadsheet makes validation much easier than sifting through pages in a requirements document. A spreadsheet is an extremely unambiguous way to represent the sourcing requirements. Once the concept source is validated and agreed upon, the Concept Family Tree is still useful as a reference. Long after the application is developed and in production, people will still need to refer to this information. Table 9.3 contains an example of a Concept Family Tree.

Table 9.3 – Sample Concept Family Tree

From Here				To Arrive Here		
Name	Source	Definition	History	Name	Definition	History
Customer	Customer Reference Database	The recipient and purchaser of our products.	10	Customer	The recipient and purchaser of our products.	3
Order	Order Entry	A contract to buy a quantity of product at a specified price.	4	Order	A contract to buy a quantity of product at a specified price.	3
Item	Item Reference Database	Anything we buy, sell, stock, move, or make. Any manufactured or purchased part, material, component, assembly, or product.	10	Product	Anything we buy, sell, stock, move, or make. Any manufactured or purchased part, material, component, assembly, or product.	3
Party	Data Warehouse	A person or company that is important to our business in some way.	5	Associate	A person who is employed in a full or part time capacity by our company, to perform a service or function to our company.	3
Time	Data Warehouse	A measurable length of seconds, minutes, hours, days, weeks, months or years. Can include both fiscal and Julian time measurements.	10	Time	A measurable length of seconds, minutes, hours, days, weeks, months or years. Can include both fiscal and Julian time measurements.	3

Here is a description of each of the columns in this spreadsheet:

- **Name**. This column contains the names of all the concepts within the application. If a concept is left out of this document, there is a good chance that it will not be modeled in the concept modeling phase, and therefore will probably not appear in the logical or physical data model, either. So if Account is left out of this document, it may not be included within the scope of the application. The Name on the source set of columns is often more generic than the Name on the receiving set of columns. For example, Party is the source for Associate information.
- **Source**. This column contains the name of the application that provides the data for each concept. Note that a source application is not just limited to a database, but can also be a file or a spreadsheet. A very important question to answer at this point is "How far should I go back?" That is, should we list all of the source applications until we reach the point where a user is typing the information in? Or should we just go back to the immediate source? My advice is to continue following the concept upstream until you arrive at a reliable and accurate source for this concept, and then stop. Let's say we have Customer as a concept in our family tree and that it's for a data mart. If the concept currently exists in the data warehouse, this should be our reliable and accurate source, and therefore we should stop here. So for customer, in this example, we only need to go back one application to the data warehouse.
- **Definition**. Just as we have seen with the Name column, we can have multiple definitions for a single concept on this tree. The destination definition, or definition that we are modeling, should be consistent with the enterprise definition finalized during the Concept List. However, there is a small but possible

chance that one of the source systems might have a definition slightly different than the enterprise definition. Therefore, we need to capture this to make sure we have identified the correct source.

- **History**. The History column under the source set of columns is the number of years of history the system has on this concept. For example the XYZ source system might have two years of history. The History column under the "To Arrive Here" column, meaning for the one you are modeling, is how much history we need. This is a very important distinction. If we want more history than we have in our source system, then we have an issue and must work with our users to agree on less history, at least in the beginning. Finding this history gap at the concept level could catch a potentially serious problem very early on and before much time has been invested in this project. It also will help set the user's expectations. This column is optional for operational applications yet mandatory for business intelligence applications.
- **Questions and Impact**. Because so many people might be looking at this spreadsheet, and this might be the first time the source information has been viewed in this format, there will probably be many questions and comments. Questions and comments must be addressed at the concept level, since answering a question at this level can save problems later on.

The Concept Family Tree, although rarely more than a page in length, has several objectives:

- **Captures each concept's source applications.** The Concept Family Tree contains each of the applications that play a role in transporting and shaping the content of each of the concepts. Not only does this tree list the applications that sourced this concept, it also identifies any major impacts the application has on this concept.

- **Determines impact on existing application architecture.** The Concept Family Tree will identify new interfaces that will need to be developed. These new interfaces impact the upstream applications, and therefore impact the current application architecture. For example, if the new application we are working on is a data mart, the Concept Family Tree will identify what concepts currently exist within the data warehouse that can be reused, which concepts will need some type of enhancement, and which new concepts will have to be brought into the data warehouse. This gives a high-level understanding of the impact from each required concept.
- **Estimates work effort.** Before starting development, you can gauge pretty accurately how much effort it would take to get the information required. You can judge how many applications are involved and the impact each application will have on your development and vice versa. This allows you to create an estimate at the concept level of the effort it will take to bring this new information into the application. We usually recommend filling in this spreadsheet before finalizing the work estimate. Note that if we are developing a data mart, we cannot complete a concept level estimate until the Concept Grain Matrix, described next, is also complete.
- **Identifies sourcing issues early.** By determining the sources at the concept level, you could potentially save a lot of frustration and time by identifying a sourcing issue at this early stage. For example, let's say your users want three years of history for Customer and by filling in the Concept Family Tree, you realize that the source system only keeps one year of Customer history. This is a problem that you have discovered with a minimal amount of analysis and time. Identifying problems like this one early on is a great benefit of this tool. It takes a proactive approach to sourcing issues.

Concept Grain Matrix

The Concept Grain Matrix is a spreadsheet that captures the levels of reporting for each concept or fact. It is the spreadsheet view of a dimensional HDM. This spreadsheet view provides a universal translator between business users and the technical project team. Both business users and the project team can understand and validate the reporting requirements through this spreadsheet. Business users might 'speak' the language of reports, whereas technical people might 'speak' the language of dimensional models. The Concept Grain Matrix is a common ground; a spreadsheet that both users and technical people can relate to and use as a medium for communication. Note that this is only for dimensional reporting applications. Any application that has heavy reporting requirements can take advantage of this tool.

The Concept Grain Matrix can be used for both ad hoc and standard reporting. In ad hoc reporting, the user has greater access to data and the types of queries they can execute. Standard reporting includes predefined queries the user can execute with limited access to the data. Standard reports usually contain fairly summarized information. They are formatted to the user's specifications, with enough of the details hidden to make standard reporting more manageable and understandable to the average user. Ad hoc reporting, on the other hand, is pretty much direct access to the database tables and is therefore more complex. It requires greater understanding of the underlying structures. For example, a standard report might be the monthly profit report by customer. An ad hoc report might start out with a similar monthly report but then the user might want to select different data elements to report on monthly promotions by customer, monthly complaints by customer, and so on.

The Concept Grain Matrix can meet both ad hoc and standard reporting needs, usually with separate matrices or different notations on the same matrix. There are even times when each standard report might require its own Concept Grain Matrix or different notation on the same matrix.

Table 9.4 contains the Concept Grain Matrix after having been filled in initially. Note the different notation used for ad hoc versus the production and shipments summary standard reports. With ad hoc analysis, if a dimension is referred to, it is usually at the lowest level. For example, ad hoc analysis of Product will always be at the Product level.

Table 9.4 – Sample Concept Grain Matrix

Concept	Time				Customer		Product	
	Year	Quarter	Month	Day	Category	Customer	Brand	Item
Shipments	AB	AB	AB	A	AB	A	AB	A
Debits	A	A	A	A	A	A		
Credits	A	A	A	A	A	A		
Balances	A	A	A	A			A	A
Production	AC	AC	A	A			AC	AC
Contact	A	A	A	A	A	A	A	A

LEGEND:

A = Ad hoc reporting, B = Shipments Summary Report, C = Production Summary Report

The Concept Grain Matrix acts as a universal translator for data mart reporting requirements. The common language created on this spreadsheet by business users and the technical team accomplishes several goals:

- **Permits discussion and agreement on the levels of reporting without showing a data model.** Many users we've worked with have difficulty understanding data modeling concepts. This can cause confusion and frustration to a user when using a dimensional data model to validate reporting requirements. Rather than use the model as a validation mechanism, we prefer to use the Concept Grain Matrix. Not too long ago, we validated with a business user all of the concept reporting requirements for a financial data mart, without showing a single data model. We've found all users are very comfortable with a spreadsheet. The spreadsheet format, as we've seen with the Concept Family Tree, provides an unambiguous format for capturing the reporting requirements. Sometimes looking at report printouts or paragraphs of text in a requirements document can lead to lots of questions or incorrect assumptions. A spreadsheet more clearly displays the reporting requirements, making it easier for agreement and validation.
- **Complements the Family Tree.** The Concept Family Tree captures the source information for each concept, and the Concept Grain Matrix captures the reporting requirements for each fact or measurement concept. These two documents are tightly coupled. Without the family tree, we would never be able to validate if our reporting requirements are realistic, based on what is available in the existing applications. Without the grain matrix, we would need to add an incredible amount of redundancy to the family tree to capture all possible combinations of fact concepts with reporting levels. For example, if our grain matrix captures that we need to view sales down to a product level, we need to validate this request in the family tree by making sure the source system for sales information goes down to a product level. Likewise, sales might be viewed by item, by customer, by month, by day, etc., and each of these

different ways of viewing sales would need to appear as a separate row in the family tree document if we did not have the grain matrix to capture all these variations of sales in a single row.

- **Estimates work effort.** Before starting development, you can roughly estimate how many structures will be required in your physical design. The Concept Grain Matrix, combined with the Concept Family Tree, is a quick way to arrive at an accurate estimate for data mart development.

Industry Data Models

An industry data model is a prebuilt data model that captures how an organization in a particular industry works or should work. Industry models are not 'silver bullets'. That is, they don't remove the need for data modelers. Data modelers are still needed to interpret and expand the model.

Industry data models are almost exclusively built at a logical level of detail. This means they are all fully-attributed, very detailed, yet still independent of technology. That is, they represent a business solution and not a technical solution. The technical solution would involve techniques to boost performance and improve security for example.

In some cases the logical industry standard model also comes with a HDM. Teradata for example, offers a series of data models by industry. In their Communications industry data model, they provide a HDM, a subset shown in Figure 9.1.

Figure 9.1 – Subset of Teradata Communications Industry Data Model[5]

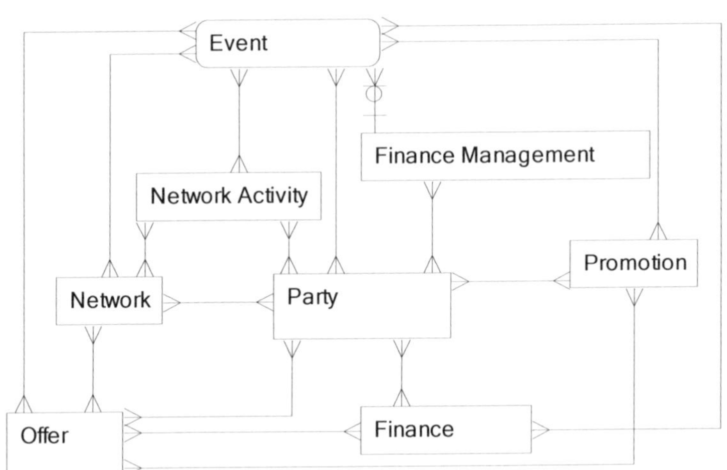

The definitions of the concepts on these models are usually fairly robust, such as this definition for Offer: "Provides information about the Products or Product Packages (Offerings) that are sold by the Communications Service Provider. Offerings may contain one or more Products. Offerings have characterizing Descriptors, such as Cost per Minute of Usage or Monthly Recurring Charge."

To give you a feel for how high-level a HDM can be, more than 100 logical entities, including Offering, Product, and Incentive, are represented by just the single Offer concept on this model. This Teradata HDM allows an organization to achieve a high-level big picture of the organization without getting overwhelmed by jumping straight into a complex logical design.

If an industry data model does not exist at a HDM level, you will find yourself doing the added step of folding up the model into a higher level. For example, you would need to perform the activity of folding 100 logical order entities into the concept

5 The Teradata Communications Industry Logical Data Model, Overview and Application, By Steve Hoberman, 2008.

Order. This is not a trivial task, as many industry data models are large in size easily spanning over 1000 entities.

There are a number of benefits an industry data model at the HDM can provide:

- **Match industry**. These models are often built with the industry in mind and not a specific organization. Therefore, if you are striving to improve information sharing with external organizations or are looking for internal consistency, you might find yourself using one of these models.
- **Resolve arguments**. If there are folks within your organization who are clashing on what to call the concept or what the concept means, it can help diffuse the argument by bringing in an external industry view. This way neither party loses—they are both agreeing on an industry standard.
- **Minimize risk**. One organization that we worked with used an industry data model for the primary purpose of minimizing the chances of missing a concept. If everything on the industry model is accounted for in a particular model, then there are no gaps in the model.

If you would like to pursue the industry standard model route to reduce the amount of time it takes to build a HDM and to match a standard industry model, there are a number of useful sources worth considering:

- **Websites:** You can search on the Web for terms such as 'Insurance Data Model' and see if any of the results can be used. Websites work best when you are planning on building your own HDM and want to supplement it or validate it with existing structures. Although this is the least expensive method of obtaining industry models, it also could be the most suspect. Data models on the internet might be outdated or in early release forms or simply incorrect. However, it can provide some useful information. One time we needed to understand how different organizations modeled the concept of Person. We found many person models on the web and were able to combine bits and pieces from many of these models to create a new model that we felt was very robust. The Internet is a great place to get definitions, using sites such as wikipedia.org and google.com. Here is a great site, for example, that offers starter data models for free: www.databaseanswers.org/data_models/index.htm.

- **Books.** There are several books on the market that could give your HDM effort a head start. Books are relatively inexpensive and at times a very useful source for a HDM. Books written by Len Silverston and David Hay (see suggested reading) could shorten the HDM modeling effort. These books provide very flexible, reusable structures that you can customize relatively easily for your business.
- **Industry organizations.** A number of industries, such as telecommunications and healthcare, have a consortium that work together on initiatives useful to all of its members. Justice departments also have joined together to produce one common way of looking at justice-related information, called the Global Justice Data Model (JXDM). The telecommunications consortium has the SID (Shared Information Data Model) and healthcare has the HL7 Reference Information Model (RIM). The National Retail Federations' Association of Retail Technology Standards (ARTS) Committee has the ARTS data model for retail.
- **Vendor models.** There are a number of vendors including Teradata, ADRM and IBM that offer extremely detailed and comprehensive data models by industry. For example, a healthcare company can purchase one of the healthcare industry data models offered by one of these vendors.

Key Points

- The In-The-Know Template captures the people and documentation that can provide and validate the data requirements
- The Concept List is a listing of the concepts the business feels are important to capture, without worrying about the terminology on a data model
- The Concept Family Tree is a spreadsheet that captures the source applications and other key metadata for each concept within the scope of our application
- The Concept Grain Matrix is a spreadsheet that captures the levels of reporting for each concept or fact. It is the spreadsheet view of a dimensional HDM.
- An industry data model is a prebuilt data model that captures how an organization in a particular industry works or should work

CHAPTER 10
Putting the Pieces Together

You are the data architect for a large ice cream manufacturer called Lots Of Ice Cream. They have just embarked on an enterprise data warehouse solution. There are a number of siloed reporting systems including Ice, which is their current sales reporting system. They want to replace this reporting system with a more robust and function-rich data mart as part of their data warehouse architecture. This new system will be called Ice Cube. (Note that 'Cube' is a popular structure for a data mart, so you know these ice cream folks have a sense of humor.)

The Ice reporting system has been around since the early 1980's and has, for the most part, satisfied business users. They understand the reports well and the system is very reliable. There is some functionality the business would like to add to Ice as well as the ability to allow business users to drill up and down within the data at their ease. Due to the amount of effort required to modify Ice with its older technology to accommodate the additional functionality and accessibility now required, it was agreed to rewrite the application completely under the new data mart Ice Cube.

We are going to build two high-level data models:

- Ice, which is the existing application
- Ice Cube, which is the proposed application

Let's walk through the ten steps for both of these HDMs, starting with Ice.

The Ice HDM

The following ten steps need to be applied to complete the Ice HDM.

STEP 1: IDENTIFY MODEL PURPOSE

We know that the Ice system has been around for quite a long time and that the users are happy with it, for the most part. Therefore, a first step towards understanding what changes they would like in the new Ice Cube application is to first understand Ice. Therefore, the purpose of our model is to communicate, at a high-level, how the existing application, Ice, works. Recall Table 8.1 which listed the four different model purposes. Table 10.1 uses this same template to illustrate which quadrant the Ice HDM fits within.

Table 10.1 – Where the Ice HDM Fits

	Existing	Proposed
Business		
Application	Ice HDM	

STEP 2: IDENTIFY MODEL STAKEHOLDERS

You'll remember Table 8.2, which describes model stakeholder roles and their definitions. For Ice, Table 10.2 highlights the small subset of these roles that will be translated into actual stakeholders. For existing legacy systems, we traditionally have more support- and user-based roles. This is because no new development work is required, so the roles are in place to keep the existing application running.

Table 10.2 – Roles which get Translated into Stakeholders for Ice

Role	Builder when purpose is to model an application	User
Business User		✓
Data Modeler	✓	✓
Project Manager for Ice	✓	✓
Project Manager for Ice Cube		✓
Support	✓	✓
Trainer		✓

In terms of builders, the data modeler will most likely lead the effort, with input from the project manager for the existing Ice application. From the business side, the key business user will also be a valuable source of input. When an existing application is being modeled, having a representative from the support team is also very useful. The support team often knows more about the internals of an application than anybody else because they have to fix it when it breaks at 3 A.M.

In terms of users, the training department will most likely use this model as a tool to educate people new to the team. The project manager for Ice will also use the model as a communication tool with upper management and within their teams.

STEP 3: INVENTORY AVAILABLE RESOURCES

Resources include people and documentation. For people resources, we can further distinguish the business from IT resources that are available to help build the Ice high-level data model.

An In-The-Know spreadsheet was completed, as shown in Table 10.3, based on the roles identified in Step 2.

Table 10.3 – Ice HDM In-The-Know Spreadsheet

Concept	Resource	Type	Role / How used	Location/ Contact
[All]	Mary Jones	Business	Key business user who knows the existing reports better than anybody	973-555-1212, m@lotsoficec.com
[All]	John Jitterbug	IT	Data Modeler	732-555-1212, jj@lotsoficec.com
[All]	Max Smith	IT	Ice Project Manager	212-555-1212, ms@lotsoficec.com
[All]	Bill Francis	IT	Ice Cube Project Manager	516-555-1212, bf@lotsoficec.com
[All]	Jill Johnson	IT	Support Team Member	206-555-1212, jo@lotsoficec.com
[All]	Tom Cone	Business	Trainer	508-555-1212, tc@lotsoficec.com
[All]	Ice Support Handbook	Document	Last updated in 1986, this document brings new support people up to speed. Includes column layout.	S://public_directory/Ice/Support/ich.doc

The term '[All]' in the Concept column indicates that this resource is the contact for all subject areas, such as ice cream and inventory.

As with most legacy systems, we learn that documentation is lacking. The Ice Support Handbook appears to be the only document and it was most recently updated the last time the Mets won the World Series. It includes a column layout, but it probably will not be up-to-date.

In terms of people resources, Mary, the key business user, and Jill, the support team member, are likely to be the main sources of information for the model.

STEP 4: DETERMINE TYPE OF MODEL

The HDM needs to be one of four different variations, as shown in Table 10.4.

The grayed-in cell is the one that we will build for the Ice HDM.

Table 10.4 – Choosing Model Type for Ice HDM

	Relational	Dimensional
Business	Choose when capturing how the business works and there is a need to understand a business area, design an enterprise data model, or start a new development effort.	Choose when capturing how the business is monitored and there is a need to visually capture how the business is going to play with numbers. That is, view metrics at different levels of granularity, such as by Month and Year.
Application	Choose when capturing how the application works and there is a need to understand an existing or proposed application, or start a new development effort.	Choose when capturing how the business is monitored through a particular application. The application allows users to view metrics at different levels of granularity, such as by Month and Year.

The reason that we need a relational model is the existing reporting system is relational. A relational data model encompasses the data and rules of the *execution* of a business process. Most legacy reporting applications are built using relational modeling techniques. On a high-level model, the lines retain this function, capturing high-level rules between the different concepts.

We also need it to have an application view, as our goal is to understand this existing application. An application perspective is a high-level model of a defined portion of a particular application. This perspective is for the existing Ice application.

STEP 5: SELECT APPROACH

There are support people who understand the existing application environment, as well as enthusiastic business people who know the system very well from an end-user perspective. Therefore, there are ample people resources. Having IT people who know the existing system leans us more towards a bottom-up approach. In addition, the key business user knows the system well from the reporting and functional side, giving further strength to proceeding bottom-up. The bottom-up approach temporarily ignores what the business needs and instead focuses on the existing systems environment. We build an initial high-level data model by studying the systems that the business is using today.

STEP 6: COMPLETE AUDIENCE-VIEW HDM

There are a number of different application structures to lean on to start the information gathering stage. The most popular is the existing database, which can automatically be reverse-engineered in most data modeling tools. This means the data modeling tool can simply 'point' to the database and extract it up into boxes and lines.

Unfortunately for us, the Ice reporting system is in a legacy database technology that can no longer be reversed-engineered. Therefore, we have to rely on our documentation, at least for the first cut model. The Ice Support Handbook contains the 1986 list of database columns. A subset is shown in Figure 10.1.

Figure 10.1 – Ice Support Handbook List of Database Columns (Subset Shown)

```
FlavrName

FlavrCode

FlavrFirstIntroducedDate

FlavrIdealTemperature

Daily_produced_gallons

Daily_inventory_gallons
```

We should be very cautious with this list. There may be some inaccuracies between the documentation and the existing production Ice reporting system. But this list of database columns provides a good starting point.

We can also examine existing reports and interface layouts to produce the bottom-up model. Mary Jones, the key business user, walks John, the data modeler, through the two reports produced by the Ice reporting system, showing him two sample reports, as shown in Figure 10.2.

Figure 10.2 – Two Sample Reports

Amount of Ice Cream Produced in Hundred Gallons for Last Four Quarters

Flavor	Most Recent Quarter	Most Recent Quarter - 1	Most Recent Quarter - 2	Most Recent Quarter - 3
Chocolate	56	63	34	72
Vanilla	53	59	32	68
Strawberry	35	30	25	41
Pickles-n-cream	9	7	5	3

Amount of Ice Cream Remaining in Inventory in Hundred Gallons for Last Four Quarters

Flavor	Most Recent Quarter	Most Recent Quarter - 1	Most Recent Quarter - 2	Most Recent Quarter - 3
Chocolate	15	21	19	21
Vanilla	10	21	19	30
Strawberry	0	0	0	2
Pickles-n-cream	9	7	5	2

The users examine these two reports to determine how much product is sold, as well as what flavors to produce more of and what flavors to produce less of. For example, it appears that Strawberry has almost no inventory; therefore more will need to be made next quarter. However, Pickles-n-cream has only sold one hundred gallons these past four quarters so maybe the company should stop producing it.

There are no Sales reports, so the users rely on these two reports plus their own knowledge of how things work to derive sales. (I guess we can understand why they need a new system.) For example, by subtracting inventory from what was produced one can get a very rough idea of what was sold. Seasoned business experts can adjust these rough figures for events such as returns and spoiled products (something tells me Pickles-n-cream is going to wind up spoiled).

From all of these resources, the modeler produced an initial HDM. Meetings with the IT resources who support the existing application were held, as well as meetings with the business users who understand the system well from a reporting perspective. The modeler was able to update and then validate the model using this approach.

Building a starter model prior to meeting with the IT and business resources proved to be a valuable timesaver, as the starter model represented a very close depiction of the actual system.

Figure 10.3 contains the Ice audience-view HDM.

Figure 10.3 – Ice Audience-View HDM

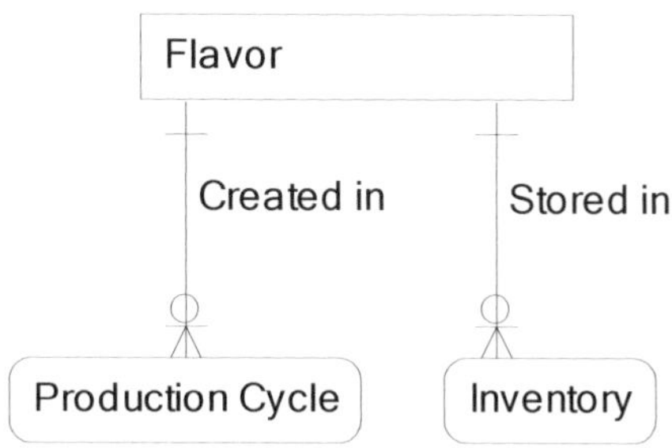

Concept definitions:

Flavor – One distinguishes the taste of one ice cream product over another. Flavors are recognized by consumers and examples include Chocolate, Vanilla, and Strawberry.

Inventory – The storage quantity of a particular ice cream flavor in our warehouse on a given day. Currently we have only one warehouse.

Production Cycle – The quantity of a particular ice cream flavor produced on a given day.

Business Rules (listed in the order we would typically walk someone through the model):

- Each Flavor can be created in many Production Cycles.
- Each Production Cycle must be performed for one Flavor.
- Each Flavor can be stored in many Inventories.
- Each Inventory must store one Flavor.

STEP 7: INCORPORATE ENTERPRISE TERMINOLOGY

Once there is agreement from the stakeholders that the correct view of their world is captured in the boxes and lines of the high-level model, we now need to make sure the model you have built is consistent with other terminology within the organization. Another way of saying this is that now that the model is correct (Step 6), make sure the model is consistent (Step 7) with the rest of the organization.

Lots Of Ice Cream does not have an enterprise data model. However, they do have many business experts who have broad backgrounds and have worked at the company for many years. John Jitterbug, the data modeler, met with each of these experts. Most of the meetings took place in one-on-one sessions, where John met with only one expert at a time. John's goal was to ensure the terms and definitions on this Ice HDM are consistent with the understanding of these company experts. Where there were discrepancies between terms or definitions,

John organized bigger working groups to resolve the issues. Figure 10.4 captures the enterprise-view model for Ice.

Figure 10.4 – Enterprise-View of Ice

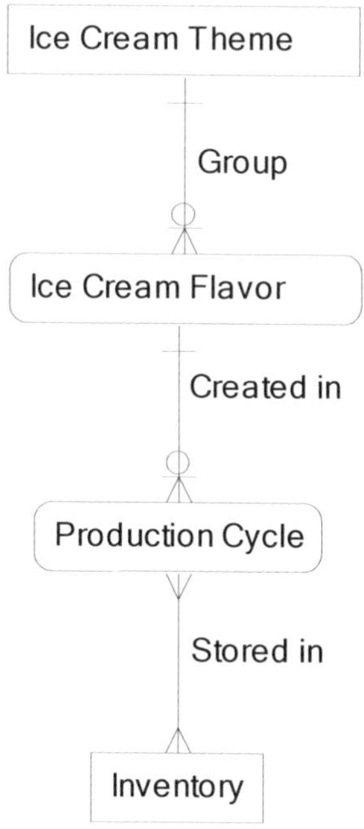

Concept definitions:

Ice Cream Flavor – One distinguishes the taste of one ice cream product over another. Flavors are recognized by consumers and examples include Chocolate, Vanilla, and Strawberry.

Ice Cream Theme – A collection of ice cream flavors that have been grouped together because they share at least one common property. For example, the Brownie Ice Cream and Cake Batter Ice Cream flavors are grouped into the Cake Ice Cream Theme.

Inventory – The quantity of a particular ice cream flavor stored in our warehouse on a given day. Currently we have only one warehouse.

Production Cycle – The quantity of a particular ice cream flavor produced on a given day.

Business Rules (listed in the order we would typically walk someone through the model):

- Each Ice Cream Theme can group many Ice Cream Flavors.
- Each Ice Cream Flavor must belong to one Ice Cream Theme.
- Each Ice Cream Flavor can be created in many Production Cycles.
- Each Production Cycle must be performed for one Ice Cream Flavor.
- Each Production Cycle must be stored in many Inventories.
- Each Inventory must store many Production Cycles.

Note that there were quite a few passionate discussions when transitioning from the audience-view to this enterprise view.

For example, over two weeks were spent debating whether 'Flavor' or 'Ice Cream Flavor' was the right term. The key business user for the Ice reporting system emphasized that everyone in her area just calls it 'Flavor'. However, business experts from different parts of the business said confusion could arise because there are different types of products each with their own flavor, such as Sprinkle Flavors. After several meetings with different groups, there was consensus on the term 'Ice Cream Flavor'.

There also were debates on how Inventory relates to Ice Cream Flavor, with the consensus being that Inventory relates to Production Cycle and not directly to Ice Cream Flavor.

STEP 8: SIGNOFF

Due to the simplicity of the model, signoff on the Ice HDM was an easy step. The stakeholders involved in building the model were asked to sign off on the model, and because of their involvement, signoff was a non-event. There was one meeting where everyone was invited and the data modeler walked through the model one final time. After a minor discussion or two with the audience, the model was deemed complete and correct. The meeting ended with a cheerful pizza party.

STEP 9: MARKET

This model was marketed through a series of lunch-and-learn programs where free lunch and Pickles-n-cream ice cream for dessert was provided as a way to entice employees to come learn about the model. After all, there really isn't such a thing as a free lunch anymore, is there?

STEP 10: MAINTAIN

The model required no maintenance as it represented an application that was being replaced by the Ice Cube application. Therefore, once this model was signed off, it was considered to be frozen and became the starting point for the Ice Cube HDM.

The Ice Cube HDM

The Ice HDM is a great starting point for the new application HDM, Ice Cube. Here are the ten steps for building the Ice Cube HDM.

STEP 1: IDENTIFY MODEL PURPOSE

Ice Cube is the replacement for Ice. The goal for modeling Ice Cube at a high-level is to communicate how this proposed application should work. The HDM is a very good place to start capturing the concepts and business rules for a new application. This way terminology, rules, and definitions can be agreed upon prior to detailed project analysis. It will save time, money and unpleasant surprises further down in the software lifecycle. Recall Table 8.1, which listed the four different model purposes. Table 10.5 uses this same template to illustrate on which quadrant the Ice Cube HDM fits.

Table 10.5 – Where the Ice Cube HDM Fits

	Existing	Proposed
Business		
Application		Ice Cube HDM

STEP 2: IDENTIFY MODEL STAKEHOLDERS

Recall that Table 8.2 described model stakeholder roles and their definitions. The chart in Table 10.6 summarizes these roles and identifies which roles typically build and use the HDM.

Table 10.6 – Roles Which Get Translated into Stakeholders for Ice Cube

Role	Builder when purpose is to model an application	User
Business User		✓
Data Modeler	✓	✓
Business Analyst	✓	✓
Project Manager	✓	✓
Support	✓	✓
Trainer		✓

In terms of builders, the data modeler will most likely lead the effort, with input from the project manager for the new Ice

Cube application. From the business side, the key business user for the new application (and/or project sponsor) will also be a valuable source of input.

In terms of users, the training department will probably use this model as a tool to educate people new to the team. The project manager and project sponsor for Ice Cube will also use the model as a communication tool with upper management and within their teams.

STEP 3: INVENTORY AVAILABLE RESOURCES

For people resources, we have knowledgeable business people who know what they want from the new system. Unfortunately, it shouldn't come as any surprise that there is only a one-page functional requirements document. Over the last decade, written requirements have shrunk in length from over 100 pages, on average, to just about what fits cleanly on a coffee-stained restaurant napkin. The requirements still exist; they are just not documented as much as a decade ago. This puts more emphasis on the data model to capture the precise requirements.

Table 10.7 contains the completed In-The-Know spreadsheet for the Ice Cube HDM.

Table 10.7 – Ice Cube HDM In-The-Know Spreadsheet

Concept	Resource	Type	Role / How used	Location / Contact
Ice Cream Flavor	John Bonnet	Business	Business analyst on ice cream flavors	444-555-1212, jb@lotsoficec.com
Ice Cream Themes	Richard Fish	Business	Business analyst on ice cream themes	555-555-1212, rf@lotsoficec.com
Inventory &Production	Janet Viola	Business	Business analyst on inventory and production	121-555-1212, jv@lotsoficec.com
[All]	Mary Jones	Business	Key business user who knows the existing reports better than anybody. She will also be the key system user.	973-555-1212, m@lotsoficec.com
[All]	John Jitterbug	IT	Data modeler	732-555-1212, jj@lotsoficec.com
[All]	Bill Francis	IT	Ice Cube Project Manager	516-555-1212, bf@lotsoficec.com
[All]	Jill Johnson	IT	Support Team member	206-555-1212, jo@lotsoficec.com
[All]	Tom Cone	Business	Trainer	508-555-1212, tc@lotsoficec.com
[All]	Ice Cube Functional Requirements	Document	One page documentation. Will need to supplement this with lots of meetings with the key business user.	S://public/IceCube/icfr.doc

STEP 4: DETERMINE TYPE OF MODEL

The HDM needs to be one of four different variations, as shown in Table 10.8.

The grayed-in cell is the one that we will build for the Ice Cube HDM.

Table 10.8 – Determine Type of Model for Ice Cube HDM

	Relational	Dimensional
Business	Choose when capturing how the business works and there is a need to understand a business area, design an enterprise data model, or start a new development effort.	Choose when capturing how the business is monitored and there is a need to visually capture how the business is going to play with numbers. That is, view metrics at different levels of granularity, such as by Month and Year.
Application	Choose when capturing how the application works and there is a need to understand an existing or proposed application, or start a new development effort.	Choose when capturing how the business is monitored through a particular application. The application allows users to view metrics at different levels of granularity, such as by Month and Year.

The reason we need a dimensional model is because the proposed application is for numbers-based reporting. Questions that return data elements that can be mathematically manipulated require a dimensional model. We also need it to have a business view, since our goal is to understand the proposed business reporting requirements. This view uses business terminology and rules. The model represents an application-independent view.

STEP 5: SELECT APPROACH

For this application it makes sense to use the hybrid approach. We will start off with a bit of top-down analysis and then perform some bottom-up analysis, going back and forth until the model is complete.

We will start with the top-down approach, which focuses on a purely business needs perspective. We learn how the business works and what is needed from the business people, either through direct meetings with the business, or indirectly through requirements documents and reports. Once we understand what the business is looking for in their new application, we can see how much is available in the existing Ice application. We do this by incorporating the bottom-up HDM built in the prior exercise.

We can perform a gap analysis between the Ice HDM and the new requirements to determine what needs to be added in the Ice Cube HDM.

STEP 6: COMPLETE AUDIENCE-VIEW HDM

There is very little known about the new Ice Cube application. The first step, then, is for John Jitterbug, the data modeler, to facilitate the project kickoff meeting where project team members can formally meet each other and learn about the Ice Cube requirements.

John was able to complete three deliverables on the white board during a very interactive and productive meeting, primarily through input from the three business analysts and the key business user.

While at the board sketching boxes and asking questions, he learned that Ice Cube will be a reporting application that allows the business to report gross sales for each ice cream flavor, for each state, for each month.

Table 10.9 contains the Concept Grain Matrix for the Ice Cube application. This spreadsheet provides an easy-to-read means of understanding the levels of detail (the columns) and the measures (the rows).

Table 10.9 – Ice Cube Concept Grain Matrix

Concept	**Time**		**Product**		**Sales Organization**
	Year	Month	Theme	Flavor	State
Gross Sales	X	X	X	X	X

Here are some of the questions that were asked:

- What do you do? (open-ended question to start the communication process)
- How do you define Ice Cream Flavor? How does it differ from Theme? (definition questions)
- Do you ever want to report on a geographic region other than 'State'? (scope question)
- Do you care at all about toppings, such as hot fudge and caramel? (scope question)

After investing time discussing these questions and others with the business, John comes up with the initial model, shown in Figure 10.5.

Figure 10.5 – First-Cut HDM for Ice Cube (Dimensional)

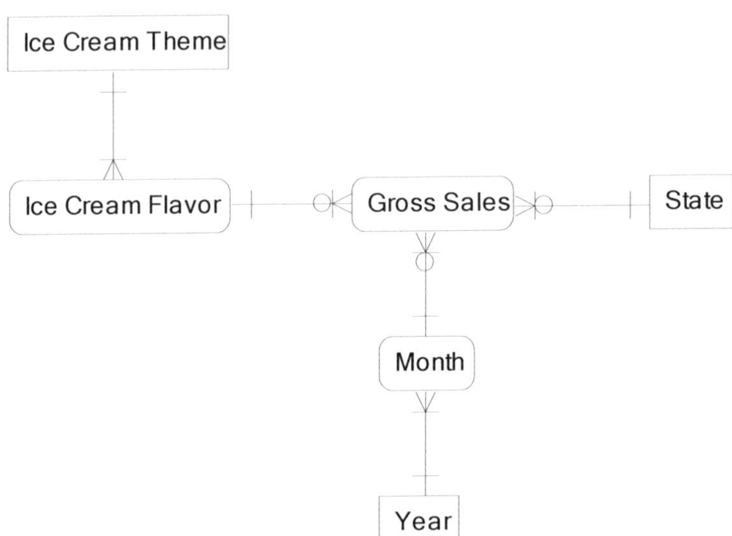

Concept definitions:

Gross Sales – The total dollar amount charged for all goods or products sold or distributed. Also included in gross sales is sales tax. Returns from melted ice cream are not deducted.

Ice Cream Flavor – One distinguishes the taste of one ice cream product over another. Flavors are recognized by consumers. Examples include Chocolate, Vanilla, and Strawberry.

Ice Cream Theme – A collection of ice cream flavors that have been grouped together because they share at least one common property. For example, the Brownie Ice Cream and Cake Batter Ice Cream flavors are grouped into the Cake Ice Cream Theme.

Month – A time unit of approximately 30 days.

State – A subset of the United States. One of the fifty states.

Year - A period of time containing 365 (or 366) days.

Navigation paths (listed in the order a user would typically navigate through the model):

"I need to see Gross Sales for each Theme and Year. If there are any surprises, I will need to drill down into the details. That is, drill down from Theme to Flavor, from Year to Month, and add State to my queries."

Notice that with a dimensional model, the focus is more on navigation than on business rules, as in a relational model.

Both the Ice Cream Flavor and Ice Cream Theme definitions have been borrowed from the Ice HDM. This is because the same team worked on both models and these definitions have already been through a critical review with experts around the company, so why reinvent them?

This model was actually built using the hybrid approach. A major source of input to the meetings was the bottom-up Ice HDM. This model was reconciled with the top-down grain matrix to produce the model in Figure 10.5.

STEP 7: INCORPORATE ENTERPRISE TERMINOLOGY

John then met with the same group of business experts with whom he met when building the Ice HDM to reconcile differences between this group and the Ice Cube team. The completed model is shown in Figure 10.6.

Figure 10.6 – Ice Cube HDM with Enterprise Terminology

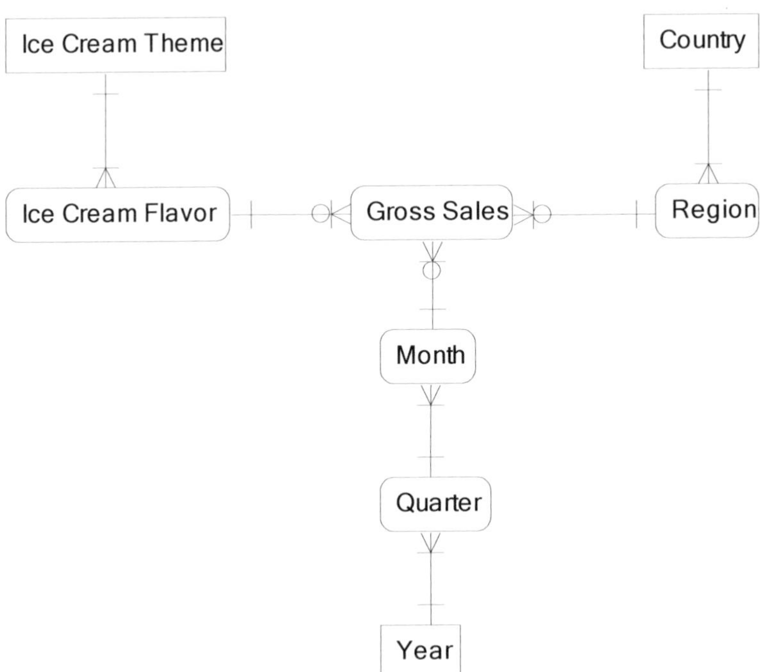

Notice that the business experts from areas outside of Ice Cube recommended that State be replaced with Region and Country. This anticipates that sometime in the future, ice cream sales reporting might be global instead of just within the United States. Also, Quarter was added between Year and Month. Here are the definitions for the three new terms on this model:

Country - A politically organized body of people under a single government.

Quarter - One of four periods into which the calendar year is divided.

Region – A geographic boundary defined by the business that rolls up into a country. Regions can be defined based on sales or governments. For example, the Northeast region.

STEP 8: SIGNOFF

The review stage took the form of several meetings. Due to the heavy involvement of the project team during the building of the HDM, there were no issues and just a few more comments that needed to be added to several of the concept definitions.

STEP 9: MARKET

There were two main marketing techniques used to promote the Ice Cube HDM. On the front page of Lots Of Ice Cream's quarterly newsletter was a picture of the HDM from Figure 10.6, with the accompanying definitions and business rules documented later in the newsletter. Not only did this get the word out on this model, it also led to several new HDM projects as managers found the model easy to read and extremely valuable for communication.

The second technique was more focused marketing directed at the IT group. This was done by printing color posters of the HDM that could be attached to cubicle walls and office doors. IT people seem to love these types of architectural posters to decorate their cubicles. However, the IT folks who are used to much more detail initially found these displayed models uncomfortable. "Where are the database tables?" was a question asked more than once in the halls upon seeing this model. Eventually, through education, even the most technical resources embraced the high-level model.

STEP 10: MAINTAIN

The logical data modeling process started with the HDM. New information was fed back to the HDM during and after the logical data modeling process to keep the models in synch. An early step in Lots of Ice Cream's methodology required the logical data modelers to start with the HDM. Later, in development, there was a step where any new findings on the logical data model were fed back into the HDM to keep it current and valuable.

Key Points

- The data model audience and the available resources have a major impact on the approach taken to build the HDM
- There are many useful templates, such as the In-The-Know template, that can save time when building the HDM and produce a higher quality data model
- Although the completed HDM may look simple, quite a bit of effort from both business and IT is required to produce such a 'simplistic' view

CHAPTER 11
Justifying a Data Modeling Tool for the High-Level Data Model

This chapter will explain the five reasons why robust data modeling tools are often needed when building the High-Level Data Model, and then using the High-Level Data Model to drive more detailed designs.

Figure 11.1 captures the first data modeling tool.

Figure 11.1 – First Data Modeling Tool

Why should we be considering modeling tools for these models? Won't a drawing tool such as PowerPoint or pencil and paper suffice? Well of course, if only a picture is required, then PowerPoint or for that matter pencil and paper can indeed be used. But if we need the ability to not only record the diagram image, but also to add vital metadata to the model, then a modeling tool is the right vehicle for this.

There are 5 fundamental reasons why modeling tools are preferable to a 'drawing' tool:

1. Metadata
2. Reuse
3. Linking
4. Impact Analysis
5. Automation

Metadata

As we've stated above, there is more to a high-level data model than just the picture. A concept such as 'Person' in a high-level data model might appear as a box on a diagram, while the relationships between concepts might appear as lines between the boxes. But there's more information about the concept than just its name, and the 'lines' show information that's important for impact analysis, information sharing, etc. If you remember our definition in Chapter 3, metadata describes the context of the information in your model. This can be text-based or expressed as relationships to other areas.

Common types of metadata that are captured for high-level data models include:

- **A business definition:** Throughout this book we've stressed the importance of having a clear business definition for every concept on your high-level data model.
- **The data 'owner' or 'steward':** The individual who is responsible for making sure that the definitions of the concept are correct and up-to-date.

- **Data quality metrics:** How well the model matches the actual data. If we've defined an attribute as an identifier, are the values unique in the actual data itself?
- **Security classifications:** Is the data related to this concept sensitive or confidential? Who is allowed to see which information?
- **Department(s) using this information:** What other departments or regions use this concept? Knowing who is using the information can be invaluable in seeking agreement on term names and definitions.
- **Language flags or alternate terms for different languages:** Is this term used in the US only? Does the UK use a different term? Do we have a translated name for the French office?
- **Status:** For example, has this name and definition been 'approved' for corporate-wide use? Is it still 'in-review'? Has it been 'phased out' and is no longer used?

It is important that any tool you choose have the ability to capture additional metadata about the objects on your model beyond the picture itself.

Reuse

One of the main goals of a high-level data model is to promote communication and information integration throughout the organization. But if we want people to use our common definitions, we have to store them where people (and tools) can access them. Good modeling tools should enable design objects including the diagrams and the metadata to be stored in accessible, searchable repositories.

But in this context just what is a repository? A repository is a place where something is deposited for safekeeping. There are several 'flavors' of repositories on the market. For simplicity's sake, we'll group them into two main types.

- **Data Model Repositories**. Data model repositories are a centralized storage point for data models. These are a great way to share model artifacts across the organization to promote reuse. For example, if you've created a standard definition for 'Customer', new modeling projects can simply take this standard from the model repository and use it in their models, rather than 'reinventing the wheel' or perhaps creating non-standard objects for their projects. In addition to the ability to share and reuse models and model concepts such as 'Customer', these repositories normally offer change management and version control. With these features, you can 'check-out' objects from the repository while you're editing them so that others don't make conflicting changes at the same time, and you can keep track of different versions of your models and see a history of changes. As we've discussed, the metadata associated with a model is as important as the model objects themselves. Most data model repositories store metadata such as definitions. A limitation of the data model repository, however, is that it captures metadata and model information only for data models, and normally from only a single model vendor. If you want to share your model information with other areas of the company (application development, BI tools, etc.), you may wish to consider a metadata repository.
- **Metadata Repositories.** A metadata repository provides a single storage point for all of the metadata in an organization. While much of this metadata originates in a data model, there are other important types of metadata that are relevant to the organization as well: application, process, organizational, legacy system metadata, etc. Most metadata repositories have import and export capabilities with a wide range of tools and formats, so concept definitions could be reused beyond the data model. For example, the definition of 'Customer' in one HDM might be relevant to a new

program being written for the accounting department. The software developer might want to reuse this definition rather than create her own. While some metadata repositories do have change management and versioning capabilities, their focus is on managing metadata, not data models, so they are not a good choice for day-to-day model management for your HDM.

In short, a way of distinguishing between these two repository types is:

- A data model repository's main purpose is to manage the change and revision of models. It may have some metadata reporting capabilities around data model-specific metadata.
- A metadata repository's main purpose is to manage and report on metadata. It has limited capabilities for managing the change and revision of data models.

Why is a repository important?

One of the biggest issues plaguing the data modeling profession is the 'not invented here' (NIH) syndrome. Too many modelers have the view that the answer to any problem is to develop a new model. Remember, sharing and re-use is a good thing!

In most businesses, many data concepts are common across business areas. Sure there may be a few minor differences, but the core concepts are, by and large, common. So why do we see people re-inventing concepts such as Person, Location, and Product for each and every model in their corporation? Modeling tools and repositories give us the ability to identify the concepts already defined, and reuse them where appropriate. Additionally, data models external to a particular organization such as Industry Standards Models or Template models can be leveraged when they are made available via a repository.

Linking

Reuse alone isn't the main reason for having a flexible repository of models. Once a model, or even a component of a model, has been reused, it would be great to know from where it originated and if there are now any differences between the original and the reused concept. After all, didn't we say that minor differences may exist?

There are two types of linking: inheritance and mapping:

- **Inheritance:** Inheritance linking shows how objects relate to each other in the design-layer hierarchy that we discussed in Chapter 3.
- **Mapping:** Mapping shows how variations of the same concept with the same semantic meaning relate to each other and usually to an agreed standard view. Table 11.1 contains an example of four HDMs that all have the same concept of Customer. We might use the term 'Customer' in the Enterprise HDM, but Sales might use the term 'Client' in their HDM. They can be semantically the same thing, but have different names. These mappings can be made both within the same modeling layer and between modeling layers.

Table 11.1 – Very Simplified View of Customer Mapping

Agreed standard source	Agreed concept name	Source	Source concept name
Enterprise HDM	Customer	Sales HDM	Client
		Consumer Care LDM	Consumer
		Marketing Reporting Application PDM	PRSPT (database table name for Prospect)

Throughout this book, we use examples of how different areas of the organization use different terms for the same concept. In some cases, our goal is to standardize on a single name for the concept. In other cases, regional differences are allowed as long as we understand that we're all talking about the same concept. Either way, we want to be able to track the relationships between these concepts so that we can easily see that 'Customer' on the Enterprise HDM is the same thing as the 'Client' on the Sales HDM and 'Cliente' on the Italian team's Sales HDM. This is where the mapping link comes in handy.

We can also show this mapping visually. In Figure 11.2 for example, we show how a concept on a HDM can be mapped to other concepts with the same semantic meaning, but with a slightly different name.

Figure 11.2 – Visual Representation of the Mapping Between High-level Data Models

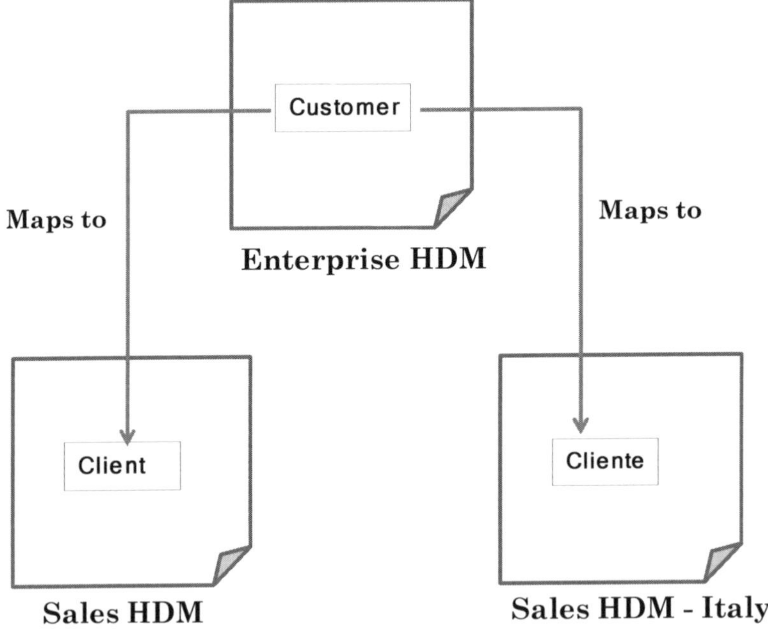

Using both inheritance and mapping links, an organization can build a body of knowledge relating to the models in which a common set of concepts (in this case Person concepts) are utilized. Thus, impact analysis (described in the next section) can be facilitated.

Impact Analysis

Within a searchable, flexible repository-based modeling tool, it should be straightforward to perform impact analysis. As we discussed in Chapter 3, impact analysis can show which concepts are related to another concept in order to see the affect that a change to a concept may have.

There are several variations of impact analysis, but all have the common goal of showing what might be affected if we were to change a concept in our HDM. These variations include the ability to show:

- **Where Used.** Shows how and where a concept is used by other models, programs, business units, etc. across the organization.
- **Process Interaction/CRUD.** Reporting shows how information is created, read, updated, or deleted by business processes in the organization. We discussed this in detail in Chapter 7.
- **Mapping.** Shows how concepts are semantically related to each other. Recall our earlier discussion in Linking.
- **Inheritance.** Shows how data is related between modeling layers. Recall our earlier discussion in Linking.

Automation

Finally, the use of modeling tools as opposed to simple drawing tools can provide benefits in that a series of tasks can be readily automated. Especially within a large organization, it is important to minimize the amount of work done by hand.

There are several areas where automation is important:

- **Generation of physical data structures.** Seasoned data modelers will at this point say *"oh yes, but what needs to be generated from a HDM?"* That's a fair point, but the HDM should be linked to a LDM and eventually a PDM. If your HDM lives in isolation in a drawing tool, you lose the benefit of being able to integrate the standards you create with your physical data platforms. Since it is these physical data platforms that run the applications of the organization, this is a major limitation.

- **Publishing**. While we know that data modeling is a wonderful thing ☺, not everybody in the business would want to roll their sleeves up and open a data modeling tool just to look at some of the key metadata, such as business descriptions, owners, applicable data standards and so on. The ability to publish data models and the accompanying business metadata in a user-friendly report or on a company's intranet or Share Point sites is becoming increasingly important. Business users and other non modeling specialists then have easy and convenient access to the information.
- **Model validation**. The dark art of validating a data model can, in part, benefit from automation. Complete automation is not possible. After all, how can a computer determine how well a model captures the business requirements? But a good tool can definitely assist with the process. We discussed the Data Model Scorecard® in Chapter 9. Certain areas of the Scorecard can be validated automatically by a modeling tool. These include:
    - **Naming standards.** Most leading modeling tools allow you to create and enforce naming standards within the tool.
    - **Definitions.** While it's hard for a tool to tell us whether or not a definition is 'good', it can tell us which concepts are missing definitions, an all too common occurrence. Making sure that all concepts have at least a rudimentary definition is a great first step to an acceptable definition.
    - **Verb Phrases for Relationships.** Relationships should have at least one verb phrase defined, and ideally two verb phrases, one for each side of the relationship line.

- **Structure:** We've stressed that a high-level data model does not need the robust, logic-based structure that a logical or physical data model has, but there are still structural definitions that need to be met, including linking between model layers and proper layout and design.

When model design layers (i.e. very high-level, high-level, logical, and physical) are created with a robust modeling tool, the linkages between the design layers can be captured automatically and don't need to be defined by hand. When selecting a modeling tool, make sure it has the ability to create several layers of models. Remember, as we discussed in Chapter 5, many tools use different names for a high-level model, so you might have to look for different words here. Some tools allow you to link multiple logical models together and hide detail, effectively creating a high-level data model without calling it that. Others might use the term 'conceptual data model' or another term altogether. Be flexible in the wording, but rigid in the requirement that automated linking be in place.

Also, as we've stressed throughout the book, good layout in a data model is essential. Certain automated features in modeling tools can assist with good design. These include the ability to:

- **'Hide' layers of detail:** It's important for a high-level data model to show only relevant information to the business audience. Many modeling tools have an option to show objects with the name only, just names and identifying attributes, etc.
- **Show definitions on the diagram:** Definitions are a critical piece of information about a high-level data model. Some modeling tools don't allow this to be shown on the model 'picture', however, and hide this information in property editors. Make sure that your HDM tool can show definitions on the diagram itself.

- **Change color and formatting based on model metadata:** As we discussed in the formatting section in Chapter 4, the use of color can help users understand the model better. It's a wonderful asset if a tool can automate the coloring based on model metadata. For example, using color to group subject areas within a model and the ability to show identifying attributes graphically.

Key Points

- Modeling tools are preferable to a drawing tool because of their ability to maintain information about metadata, reuse, linking, impact analysis and automation
- A repository is a place where something is deposited for safekeeping. Model and metadata repositories allow you to store models and metadata in a centralized place to promote reuse and consistency.
- There are very important activities that can be automated, including generation of physical data structures, publishing, model validation, linking between layers, and layout and design

---

CHAPTER 12
Key Data Modeling Tool Features for the High-Level Data Model

Now that you know you need a data modeling tool, let's talk about the key features of these tools that are unique to high-level data modeling. In evaluating a modeling tool, every organization is unique, so you need to keep your own priorities in mind throughout the evaluation. We've listed some of the common things to look out for in Table 12.1, but we've also included a 'Priority' column so that you can indicate which features are the most important in your organization. For example, it might be less important that business users be able to create their own models and more important that repository integration exists—this decision is up to you.

Table 12.1 – High-Level Data Model Feature Checklist

Feature	Priority	Available Y/N
Integration with other tools		
Design layers with linking capability		
Verbalization from the data model		
Sensible notation for high-level models		
Ability to capture business metadata		
Presentation of models		
Repository integration		
Ease of use for business users		

Integration with Other Tools

As we've mentioned earlier, a key reason for developing a high-level data model is to promote reuse of important concepts throughout the organization. In order to facilitate this reuse, other tools need to be able to consume the information from the HDM tool in an automated way. For example, if your business intelligence project wants to use the customer and product definitions that you've put together for their new reporting system, it would be ideal to have the ability to import the metadata into the BI tools that the team is using. Many good modeling tools on the market today have import and export capabilities for a wide range of other tools and formats. Common types of tools you might have at your site are:

- Report and query tools
- Data Warehousing Extract, Transform, and Load (ETL) tools
- Unified Modeling Language (UML) tools
- Business Process Modeling tools
- Business Office products such as Excel, Word, and Visio
- Databases
- Metadata repositories

The list will be unique to your company—you need to assess this based on your own criteria. If the tool has 500 import/export bridges, but none for the tools in use at your company, it might be a robust product, but not the right one for you.

Design Layers with Linking Capability

Design layers with linking capability means that the data modeling tool can forward engineer from data model to database or reverse engineer from database to data model, and keep a linking between the concepts in the different levels of detail. It's also important that the tool keep the objects 'linked but distinct'. That is, the names and properties of objects can be different and change between design layers, but the linkage remains intact. Some tools claim to have linking capability, but in actual implementation, if you change the name in one modeling layer, the names in the other modeling layers change as well. Make sure that these layers are truly distinct. A good tool should also have naming standards features so that you can choose to automate the way in which objects are named at different levels. For instance, you should be able to enforce the fact that an object is called 'Customer' at the HDM or logical level, but 'CUST' at the physical level.

Verbalization from the Data Model

The tool should have the capability to generate English declarative assertions about the data model, such that the assertions within the model can be printed or displayed. It's important to recognize, however, that the quality of these sentences is only as good as the quality of the labels on the relationship lines.

For example, from the model, the tool should be able to produce full English sentences such as:

- Each Person is identified by its Group Personal Identification Number.
- Each Person must have a First Name.
- Each Person must have a Year of Birth.
- Each Person may have an Authorization to Spend limit.
- A Person may be an Employee, a Consultant or a Contractor.
- A Person must be appointed to a Role.

Sensible Notation for High-Level Data Models

We described several different notations in Chapter 6. The tool you choose should have the ability to display the model in the notation that is most appropriate for your audience. Even better is the ability for the tool to switch between various notations, or export to different notations in different tools.

In addition, it's important that the tool be flexible enough to 'turn off' the detailed rules required for logical or physical data modeling. For example, it should not force you into using a detailed logical data model format for the production of a high-level data model.

Ability to Capture Business Metadata

The tool should have the capability of recording business metadata such as stakeholders and business definitions. It should also have extensibility to record a variety of other user defined business metadata and allow the mapping of similar terms and synonyms.

Presentation of Models

We discussed earlier the importance of being able to publish your model in an automated way and have the ability to automate the presentation display to accommodate a high-level data model, for example: hiding levels of detail, displaying definitions, using color effectively, etc. Make sure that the tool has the features you need to properly explain and market your high-level models.

Repository Integration

Most data model vendors offer a repository as an option or upgrade to their modeling tool. As we discussed earlier, this is a great venue for sharing model information. If you're also interested in sharing information with teams or tools outside of your modeling project, make sure that the tool can integrate with a full metadata repository as well.

Ease of Use for Business Users

Because of their simplicity and business focus, high-level data models can and should be created by business users, where appropriate. If the business users in your organization will be building these models on their own, consider how user-friendly the modeling tool you choose will be to them. If the focus of the tool is on logical and physical data modeling, it might be overwhelming to them. Business people are most likely familiar with tools like PowerPoint—does your modeling tool have the 'fancy' formatting options that this provides? Many modeling tools lag behind in usability and formatting options, since their focus has historically been on the physical generation of databases.

Now You Try It! Creating Your Criteria for a Tools Evaluation

You've been tasked with selecting a high-level data modeling tool for your organization. Use the High-Level Data Model Feature Checklist in Table 12.1 to determine which items are priorities for you. You can either use a numbering scheme (1-8), or terms such as 'high', 'medium', 'low'.

Key Points

- Before evaluating data modeling tools to build and store the HDM, create a checklist and have your stakeholders populate it so that you know what tool features are most important to them
- Business users may be interested in such features as ease of use, presentation of models, ability to capture business metadata, and verbalization from a data model
- Technical users may be interested in features like design layers with linking capability, the existence of a repository for reuse, integration with other tools, and a sensible notation for high-level models

CHAPTER 13
An Approach for Evaluating Data Modeling Tools for Your High-Level Data Model

Now that you understand the different features modeling tools offer, how can you choose the right one? This chapter describes an approach for evaluating data modeling tools. We will focus on the criteria required to build high-level data models. Naturally the criteria must be tailored for your organization's specific needs, but the items listed here will provide the basis for your specific investigation.

Try not to do what is shown in the cartoon in Figure 13.1.

Figure 13.1 – One Approach to Selecting a Data Modeling Tool

Why do we Need to Follow a Selection Method?

Within large organizations, there are often several different tools which largely meet the needs of the individual user communities. However, the corporate benefits of consistency, common approach, storage of models in searchable repositories and shared definitions can be lost with this piecemeal approach. An evaluation of data modeling tools needs to focus on corporate benefits instead of individual department benefits.

A selection cannot be effective if a features checklist contains only criteria for whether or not a product or vendor is suitable. A product that rates highly on, say, the technical evaluation criteria may not always be the best one for your particular environment. That is, other factors such as staff skill levels, hardware limitations, and attitude to risk must also be considered.

The selection must not be based solely on how 'good' a product is, but rather on how well suited it is to your company's needs. The product chosen may not necessarily be the best on the market, but it will be the one that best meets your requirements and yields the optimum benefits. Therefore, it is imperative that your organization's requirements be fully understood, documented and then prioritized. It is the core team's responsibility to highlight the implications of requirements (or sometimes lack of them) before the evaluation progresses too far.

The Outline Method

There is a ten-step approach to evaluating data modeling tools:

1. Identify your organization's requirements for a data modeling tool
2. Identify any organizational constraints
3. Tailor the evaluation criteria
4. Assign weights to the evaluation criteria
5. Compile a short list of candidate products

6. Evaluate the products
7. Apply the evaluation criteria against the products
8. Score and rank the products
9. Perform sensitivity and 'what if' analysis
10. Present the findings

Let's go through each of these steps.

STEP 1: IDENTIFY REQUIREMENTS

This first step is required to document the ***real*** requirements for VHDM and HDM support within the modeling tool. It should describe the major functions to be performed along with the frequency of their execution and the extent of their usage. You might start with the checklist from Chapter 12 as a starting point.

An indication of the importance that different users place on the various evaluation categories will start to be gained at this point and will be reflected in the weights that are assigned later, in Step 4. So, for example, if it's unlikely that there's any need to roll up lower levels of detail into higher level concepts in the model, this should not be included in the selection criteria. The degree to which decision making factors such as cost, security and flexibility are important to you must be determined, as they will have a significant influence on the products investigated.

At this point in the evaluation process, it is the responsibility of the core evaluation team lead to highlight the possible implications of particular requirements, particularly if they appear overly constraining. Likewise, the inclusion of too many 'mandatory' requirements (which frequently happens on the first pass) will, if rigorously followed, lead to the only possible outcome being a custom-made or home-grown solution. Ensure pragmatism in the requirements. The ideal tool has yet to be written, so don't make your evaluation fail at the first hurdle by including too many 'mandatory' requirements.

Key documents and deliverables from this step include:

- statement of VHDM / HDM tool requirements
- high-level functional requirements
- key decision-making criteria

STEP 2: IDENTIFY ORGANIZATIONAL CONSTRAINTS

Organizational constraints are usually closely associated with the requirements and should not need any extra investigative work over and above the initial user interviews. So, for example, if your organization follows a well-defined methodology, there's no point in choosing a HDM tool which requires learning a completely new methodology. Other typical types of organizational constraints are:

- hardware (e.g. must be able to run on XYZ platform)
- existing software (e.g. must be able to share information with XYZ system)
- operating system (e.g. must run on XYZ O/S)
- cost
- migration effort and timeframe
- risk
- staff skill levels (e.g. availability of employee or consultant resources)
- training availability

STEP 3: TAILOR THE EVALUATION CRITERIA

Following the first review of the evaluation criteria and agreement on the requirements, the evaluation criteria should be revised to provide the specific information that your organization is going to need to make its determination. All associated scoring spreadsheets need to be brought in line with the tailored questionnaires.

Key documents and deliverables from this step:

- tailored product and vendor evaluation questionnaires
- tailored, unweighted product and vendor evaluation spreadsheet(s)

STEP 4: ASSIGN WEIGHTS TO THE EVALUATION CRITERIA

The various sections, subsections and individual evaluation criterion should be assigned weights to represent their relative importance in your evaluation. This is best accomplished through open discussion and debate by the evaluation project team. Care must be taken in assembling the evaluation team to ensure representation from people who will actually be producing VHDMs and HDMs.

Key documents and deliverables from this step:

- Weighted product and vendor evaluation spreadsheet(s)

STEP 5: COMPILE A SHORT LIST OF CANDIDATE PRODUCTS

The short list of candidate products should include the products and vendors that are likely to satisfy the constraints as well as the products the project team knows will meet the critical requirements. The budget available for the investigation and the internal priority on evaluations should be considered when deciding on the length of the list. A short list of at least three products is reasonable whenever possible.

Is it appropriate to simply shortlist the key products already in use within your organization, or should some form of pre-qualification take place? If it is necessary to 'pre-qualify' vendors in advance of the main evaluation questionnaires, then a vendor pre-qualification questionnaire and briefing should be issued. Also, at this stage it is very important that a log of all correspondence with vendors is maintained. Usually, a number of vendors and contacts within them will be involved and they will certainly be in telephone and e-mail contact regularly. It is all too easy to lose track of what's been said and/or issued to whom and when.

Note: Don't forget to prepare and maintain a progress log once communications with potential vendors begins.

Key documents and deliverables from this step:

- short list of candidate products
- product elimination or exclusion reasons
- vendor pre-qualification questionnaires
- progress log for tracking status of communications with vendors

STEP 6: EVALUATE THE PRODUCTS

Evaluate the products by whatever methods you think will give you the information to fill in the evaluation criteria defined in Step 3. Vendor visits (or calls) are essential. Prior to each visit, the evaluation questionnaire should be provided to the vendor so that they have an opportunity to research all questions. They should also be given the name and phone number/email address of the primary contact person on the evaluation team to clarify any questions. It is very useful to issue the questions in electronic form (e.g. MS Word) as well as in print. This way the vendor can copy and paste the question into their answer. Vendor visits and demonstrations will be arranged and attended in this step, also. All members of the evaluation team must maintain clear records of vendor visits (or calls). Additional information can be obtained from a number of other sources as well—for example, user groups, published evaluation guides, web sites, etc.

Note: Deal with all of the vendors in an identical manner, with no preferential treatment.

Key documents and deliverables from this step:

- issued vendor questionnaires
- vendor visit reports

STEP 7: APPLY THE EVALUATION CRITERIA AGAINST THE PRODUCTS

After the time specified at the outset for vendors to complete the questionnaires, present demonstrations, etc., vendor responses can be assessed and scored. Apply the evaluation criteria to the products and score how well each one meets each evaluation point. Each member of the evaluation team should have an opportunity to discuss how they scored each product and explain why it merits a particular value. The evaluation team should produce one evaluation per product and/or vendor that represents their collective opinion. The core team must be kept fully informed and aligned on the scores, as these will influence the final product selection.

Key documents and deliverables from this step:

- updated product and vendor evaluation spreadsheet(s)

STEP 8: SCORE AND RANK THE PRODUCTS

Summarize the evaluation scores and, if more than three products were considered, produce a shorter list of at most three products. You may then want to benchmark each tool or subject it to an in-house trial. At a minimum the product should be demonstrated in-house in more detail than was previously shown during the vendor's demonstration. Ideally, you should use your own organization's data models to show how well the product performs in the user environment. From this the team can discuss what (if any) further information is required before preparing the final recommendation.

Key documents and deliverables from this step:

- in-house demonstration report
- recommendation and rationale for exclusion/adoption of products

STEP 9: PERFORM SENSITIVITY AND 'WHAT IF' ANALYSIS

By using the weighted product evaluation spreadsheets, the sensitivity of particular scored items can be assessed. If altering a few items dramatically affects the final ranking of the products, then the weighting assigned to them must be re-evaluated and changes agreed on. The impact on the details of the products in the affected areas must be clearly understood.

Key documents and deliverables from this step:

- confirmed recommendation

STEP 10: PRESENT THE FINDINGS

After all of the product details have been investigated and rechecked, the evaluation spreadsheets completed, and any benchmarks or trials conducted, the findings will need to be presented. The nature of the report and presentation of these findings must be determined at the outset of the investigation—for instance, a report, detailed benchmark timings, a list of weighted pros and cons, or a presentation package. Even if not explicitly required, an outline of the implications and next steps for use of the product should also be included in the findings.

Key documents and deliverables from this step:

- product findings summary
- evaluation spreadsheet(s)
- vendor product literature
- product pros and cons
- recommended product and implications for its use
- recommended next steps (e.g. for procurement, installation etc.)

Key Points

- The core team lead must highlight the implications of the requirements early in the selection process
- Follow the ten-step approach to evaluating each of the data modeling tools
- Deal with all of the vendors in an identical manner, with no preferential treatment
- The ideal tool has yet to be written, so don't make your evaluation fail at the first hurdle by including too many 'mandatory' requirements

CHAPTER 14
Case Study: Using VHDMs and HDMs at an International Energy Company

The organization in this case study is a very large international energy company which operates in many countries. Offices are dispersed across geographic regions, often in remote locations. As a result it was difficult, if not impossible, to get a single view of the corporate-wide information assets that drive the business, such as drilling fields, wells and their locations.

By implementing an enterprise-wide VHDM and several corresponding HDMs—and using many of the implementation steps we've outlined in this book, this previously distributed organization was able to achieve a single, centralized view of their strategic information assets. We'll explain how they were able to achieve this and we'll point out some of the key strategies they used to gain buy-in and acceptance of their models from both business people and IT. Remember, marketing your data model is as important as building it!

The Pain Point

Information management in general, and data modeling specifically, had not been managed in a consistent manner across the organization. Partly due to the scale of the company, and partly due to the decentralized culture, management of data as an asset had not been tackled in any serious, concerted manner. Data modeling, for example, was undertaken on a project-by-project basis, with no common method, tools or standards. Data modeling was often performed simply as a by-product of process modeling, usually in a silo with limited scope.

The project-focused nature and absence of a corporate repository also meant that project team members (frequently consultants) left at the project's conclusion, taking with them the intellectual knowledge of the area in which they had worked. Thus, each project always started from scratch. When they came across what should have been a common data concept (e.g. Customer or Product), since there was no corporate knowledge base of what had gone before, they were forced to re-invent the definitions and structures (with their own nuances). Furthermore, modeling efforts (where it was done at all) were conducted in multiple data modeling tools with little or no sharing of data artifacts.

As is also often the case in large organizations, there were several data-related initiatives in place that could have benefited from a high-level data model (remember back to Chapter 7 where we discussed common data-related initiatives). One of these initiatives was an Enterprise Architecture effort whose goal was to develop a single view of all IT assets throughout the organization including (most importantly in this case) the data assets. Rather than become yet another silo, this team decided to leverage other initiatives in the organization and pursue an enterprise-wide data modeling effort. Their goal was not only to obtain a single consolidated view of data, but to gain the buy-in of other data-related project initiatives such as master data management, process modeling, data governance, and application development.

Identifying Purpose, Stakeholders, and Goals

You'll remember that in Chapter 8 we discussed the ten-step strategy for implementing a successful high-level modeling project. The first step is to identify the model purpose. To this end, this Enterprise Architecture team created a vision for Information Management and evangelized it throughout the business to gain traction. The vision statement was:

> "Data and Information are effectively and efficiently managed as a **shared corporate asset** that is **easily accessible**."

The goal was to keep the vision concise but also hit the key pain points of the various stakeholders. Remember—the ninth step we identified in Chapter 8 is to market the model, but unless you identify the pain points, stakeholders, and strategy early in the process, marketing at the later stages will be difficult. If you get this right early on, marketing will be a breeze. Two key points of this concise value statement are that:

1. **Data is a shared corporate asset.** If the stakeholders see the result as valuable to them, they are more likely to participate.
2. **Information should be easily accessible.** Make it easy for people to share information. Even if people see the value of sharing information, if it costs them more time during the day, they are likely to go back to their siloed approach.

The major characteristics of the vision were to provide:

- Well-integrated, enterprise-wide global data, where appropriate
- A single view of customer and product master data major attributes
- Real-time, straight-through processing in areas of need
- An overt focus on data quality
- Business insights through greater data visibility
- Business ownership with a single point of accountability for data
- A defined IT role in providing leadership, coordination and verification

You'll see from these characteristics that the stakeholders included both business people and IT. This was key to the success of the project, as we'll discuss later on in the marketing section. Before we focus on the marketing aspect, however, let's go into some detail on the more technical and design aspects of building the high-level models in this organization.

Implementation

An enterprise architecture framework was created which identified and categorized data models at the same four levels we outlined in Figure 3.2, although the names used were different. As we mentioned, there are many names used for the VHDM and HDM in the industry. In this case, different names were used within the company, as well—with IT using one naming convention, while using a different set of terms to 'market' the model more effectively to the business community. Figure 14.1 outlines the names used for the model levels in this organization.

Figure 14.1 – Different Names for Different Audiences

	IT	Business
Very High-Level Data Model (VHDM)	Enterprise Data Model	'Picture'/ 'PowerPoint'
High-Level Data Model (HDM)	Conceptual Data Model	'Picture'/ 'PowerPoint'

In our discussions, however, we'll use the terms VHDM and HDM to be consistent with the rest of the book, as the meaning and purpose of the model levels aligns closely with these terms. Note that the names of the objects used on the VHDM and HDM in this organization are the same as we outlined earlier in the book: subject areas on the VHDM and concepts on the HDM.

THE VHDM

The energy company chose a Top-Down Approach, as they had ample business resources and their goal was to identify a high-level view of information resources as part of an enterprise architecture initiative. Since their focus was on operational data, they chose a relational model format. To this end, they began by creating a very high-level data model as a 'one-pager' view of all of the key subjects within the organization. These can be recognized as the key **nouns** of the enterprise, which are identified as **subjects** in the VHDM.

The very high-level data model was designed with communication very much in mind. The concept of a subject within the VHDM is one which was familiar to many of the senior business users in the company and why the term was chosen. See Figure 14.2 for a representation of this model.

Figure 14.2 – Energy Company VHDM

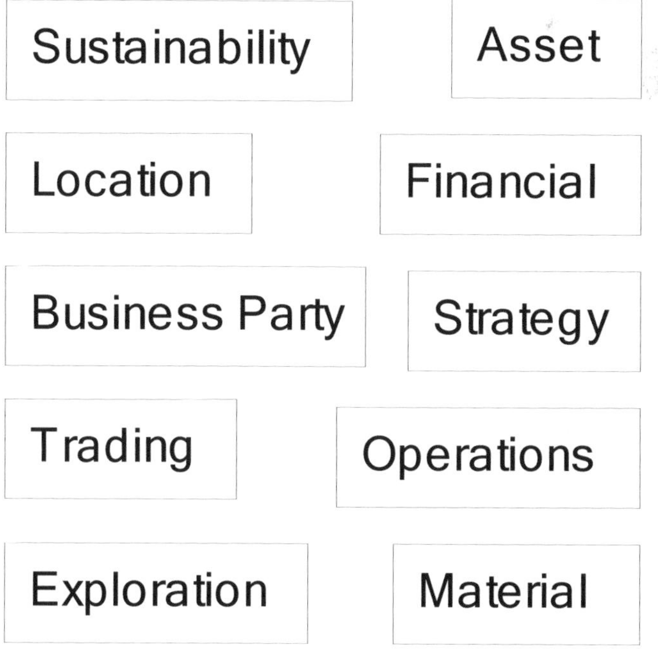

Here are definitions of three of these subjects:

- **Asset**: Assets are items with an economic value (the potential to generate cash flow) to the company, including assets not owned by the company. Assets may be tangible or intangible. Tangible assets include the various types of facilities; intangible assets include various rights that the company has acquired, such as exploration or mineral rights, or the right to emit noxious substances. The subject area includes data describing the lifecycle of assets, including maintenance records.
- **Sustainability**: "Sustainability is about achieving enduring commercial success." The company must "ensure one transaction leads to another and another". Sustainability' means the capacity to endure as a group: by renewing assets; creating and delivering better products and services that meet the evolving needs of society; attracting successive generations of employees; contributing to a sustainable environment; ensuring that future cash flows (by which the company is valued) are sustainable, and retaining the trust and support of our customers, shareholders and the communities in which we operate.
- **Exploration**: Activities necessary for the company to discover or create new productive assets. This includes searching for oil and gas by carrying out geological and geophysical surveys, followed by exploratory drilling in the most promising locations. Also includes information regarding the resulting recommendations for production.

The very high-level data model was designed to not be constrained by the current organizational structure. It was designed with three key principles in mind:

Principle 1: It must be stable (resistant to most changes in how we operate the business)

Principle 2: It must be clear (must avoid using jargon to obscure meaning)

Principle 3: It must have common meaning (i.e. be recognized and endorsed by all parts of the business, not simply one part of the business)

The VHDM was constructed for two major and complementary purposes: Communication and Governance.

- **Communication.** The very high-level data model facilitated discussion with senior business executives regarding business strategy, information ownership and stewardship, quality metrics and other such topics. The very diverse and federated nature of the business had resulted in similar terms being used in different parts of the organization to mean completely different things. Additionally, the same term was often used to mean subtly different things. Thus a key use of the very high-level data model was as a mechanism for common understanding of terms and their meaning.
- **Governance.** The very high-level data model was also used as the boundaries within which information ownership responsibilities were agreed. Since the very high-level data model is separated from organization structure, its use clearly illustrated that Information Ownership and governance was for the corporate good across the Enterprise, not simply within the bounds of one organization unit or business area.

The VHDM was not originally intended to be something directly from which a database schema or XML messages for computer systems could be built. However, further detailed high-level data models, logical data models and then physical data models built and linked to the VHDM were used for the creation of computer system components. Since the modeling tool chosen to build the VHDM was repository-based and allowed for the generation of physical databases, the work done at the business level could be reused and leveraged by IT projects as well—not only saving time and effort, but ensuring that the systems built at the 'bottom' were aligned with the vision of the business at the 'top'. This was no small feat!

THE HDM

As part of the modeling effort, the Enterprise Architecture (EA) team sought not only to identify the common subjects used across the organization, but also to identify the stakeholders, users, and other projects that were using this information. As a result of reaching out to the rest of the organization, they discovered that there was a Master Data Management (MDM) effort underway whose goal was also to create a single vision of information across the organization (see Chapter 7 for more information on MDM).

While the EA team's focus was on the VHDM-level, the MDM team's focus was on the HDM—representing the master data that is or will be shared across the entire company. Their goal was to define, model, ascribe ownership, governance and management responsibilities and procedures to corporate master data. The key examples of master data regularly encountered in the company are concepts such as: Customer, Product, Vendor, Well, Person, and Geography.

LINKING AND IMPACT ANALYSIS

These concepts aligned nicely with the subjects already defined on the VHDM. The HDM was able to go into greater detail regarding the business definitions and rules around the information. Each of the VHDM subjects can be broken down into one or more master data concepts on the Master Data HDM. The VHDM subject Financial, for example, is composed of the Master Data HDM concepts of Legal Entity, Exchange Rate and Global Financial Infrastructure. Thus, we can now see that it is possible to trace lineage from the very high-level data model through to the Master Data high-level data model. Figure 14.3 shows an example of how these model objects link together.

Figure 14.3 – Linking VHDM and HDM Model Objects

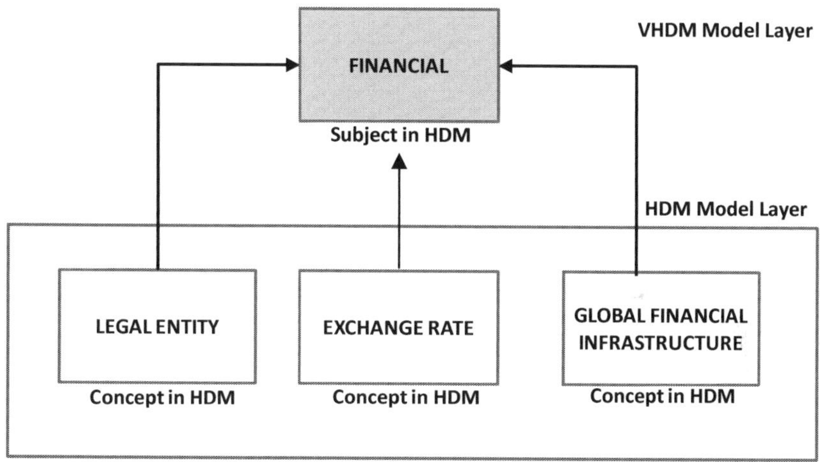

One of the major uses of the very high-level data model is Data Lineage and Impact Analysis. Not only was it possible to link the VHDM to the various concepts on the Master Data HDM, but since a repository-based data modeling tool was used, it was possible to link this information to the physical data models as well. They were then used to generate physical database structures and XML schemas.

The main questions that could be answered from the impact analysis queries based on this linking were:

- If I change this thing, what else will be affected?
- What departments or applications use this concept?
- What other terms or concepts are related to this subject?

It may be simple to answer these questions in the small example in Figure 14.3, but in this large, multinational corporate, the vast number of concepts and even larger number of physical database tables made it impossible to do this without the assistance of detailed model linkage and a repository-based system. Table 14.1 summarizes the total number of data models that currently exist, and the number planned for the future.

Table 14.1 – Numbers of Models

Model level	Number of models that currently exist	Maximum possible number of models
Very High-Level	1	1
High-Level	4	Less than 10
Logical	500+	1000+
Physical	500+	1000+

Note that there is only one very high-level data model for the Corporation. As the scope of the VHDM is Enterprise-wide, there should only be one VHDM for any organization, irrespective of its size. All of the concepts in the multiple HDMs are linked to a subject on the VHDM. There may be multiple HDMs, but the number should be small. As you reach the logical and physical levels, you can see that the number of models can be quite large—thus the need for the organizational structure defined in the VHDM and HDM to make sense of the large number of objects on the physical level.

LEVERAGING INDUSTRY DATA MODELS

In the energy sector, as in many other Industry sectors (such as Financial Services), there are several industry standard and template data models. These models were at the logical level, but they were helpful in defining some of the key concepts on the HDM. A few examples of industry data models in the energy sector include:

- PPDM – The Public Petroleum Data Model
- PSDM – Petroleum Spatial Data Model
- MIMOSA – Refinery Operations and Maintenance model (The Common Conceptual Object Model (CCOM))
- PRODML - Production Markup Language is an XML-based standard. It's used in the oil and gas industry for exchanging production data between applications.

Since these models were at the logical level, they couldn't be leveraged directly as a source for a HDM, but what they did provide was a great source for common terms and definitions. As we've discussed, achieving consensus among groups can be one of the hardest challenges in creating a HDM or VHDM—who is 'right' when it comes to finalizing on a single, enterprise-wide term? An industry standard model can be used as a 'third-party arbitrator' of sorts—taking a term or definition from an industry standard has less political baggage than choosing one department's term over the other.

Marketing

As we mentioned earlier in this case study, a vital part of the marketing effort was identifying the key stakeholders early on, understanding their pain points, and communicating the benefits of the modeling efforts throughout the process.

Let's go back to the main points in the modeling effort's vision statement:

- Data is a shared corporate asset.
- Information should be easily accessible.

To address the first point and make sure that all stakeholders, both business people and IT, saw the value of the effort and became actively involved, a series of monthly "lunch and learns" were held and a 'Modeling Community' was developed. This community was made up of business sponsors, architects and modelers. Even the modeling tool vendor was a part of the monthly meeting. Food was served to those in local offices (have we stressed enough the value of food as a motivator? ☺) and webcasts were set up for those in remote locations. Each topic focused on the benefits achieved by the various groups and regions in the Community. It was important for stakeholders to see not only their own success and achievement, but those of other groups as well. This encouraged teams to work together; in many cases, teams that had not previously been involved with modeling asked to join, subtly saying "I want my success, too!"

Sharing information via meetings was important, but equally important was making information easily accessible in the stakeholders' daily jobs. For IT, this was achieved primarily through reuse—by leveraging a common modeling tool with a shared repository, modelers could reuse objects that were already defined rather than inventing their own. This saved them valuable time and let them focus on other aspects of their job. It's human nature—if you can 'steal' work already done for you, you are likely to take that shortcut. In this case, modelers stated that they would have reused information in the past, but they (a) didn't know that other teams had this information and (b) didn't have a common format (i.e. modeling repository) to easily share the information. Once it was easy, they were happy to share.

To reach the business users, the Enterprise Architecture (EA) team needed to be more creative. In this company, many business users had been 'forced' into detailed modeling meetings that had focused on logical or physical constructs. Not surprisingly, this level of detail had them bored or confused. Now that high-level models that were more relevant to them were being used, the EA team didn't want to bring back bad memories, so they called the models 'Pictures' or 'PowerPoints'. In fact, the VHDM was formatted to look much like a PowerPoint presentation. In addition, definitions were placed in text format on the business users' intranet site. Since these users accessed this site every day for their 'regular' jobs, listing the subject and concept definitions here as 'business terms' made them both accessible and understandable.

Benefits

One of the main benefits achieved by this modeling effort was the communication and information sharing that was achieved between the groups. It was (and still is) an ongoing job to socialize the models to the Architecture community and encourage its adoption and use. To make this happen, a continuing education and coaching process is underway. The bottom line for the company has been:

"Make it easy for people to do the right thing"

Productivity aids, automation, layout templates, model validation services, and many more facilities have been delivered by the Enterprise Architecture group to make it easy for teams throughout the company to "do the right thing".

This also extends to internal marketing and publishing of the models to make it easy for users from both the business and IT to be able to read and use any or all of the model components.

Key Points

- The overall framework for Information Architecture in this international Energy Company described four levels of Data Models consistent with the four levels described earlier in the text
- Creation of one enterprise-wide very high-level data model sets the context for all Data Architecture activities within the company
- Development of a limited number of high-level data models and one Master Data High-Level Data Model enables a consistent set of data definitions to be utilized and facilitates impact analysis and data lineage
- Communication and Marketing is key to the success of the modeling effort
- Make it easy for people to do the right thing!

APPENDIX A
Answers to "Now You Try It!" Examples and Quizzes

Chapter 3
Now You Try It! Using Concepts and Relationships

The rule "A customer can have more than one account" can be expressed with the diagram below. Note that this diagram also indicates that the customer must have at least one account in order to be considered a customer. Also note we added the meaningful label name, 'own'.

Chapter 3
Now You Try It! Creating a High-Level Data Model for BI Reporting

Your high-level data model for the new reporting system should look something like this:

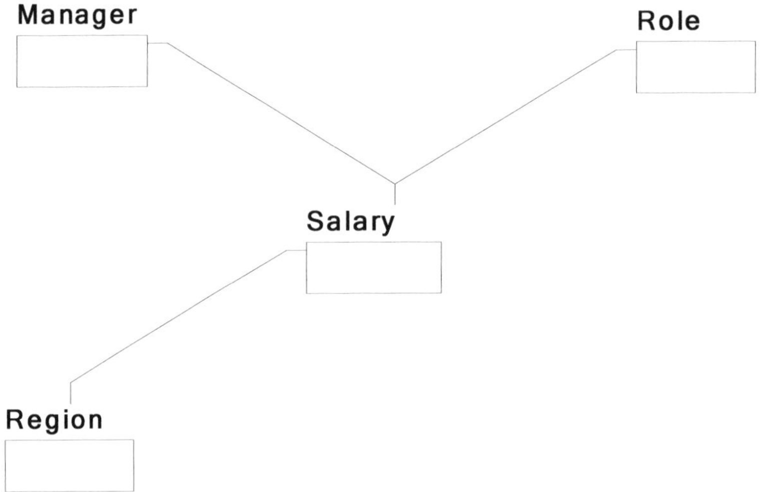

Chapter 4
Now You Try It! Understanding High-Level Data Models

Example 1:

1. A Person can declare one or many Dependents. A Dependent must be declared by one Person.
2. A child may only eat one ice cream cone. If the child does eat an ice cream cone, he will not share it.

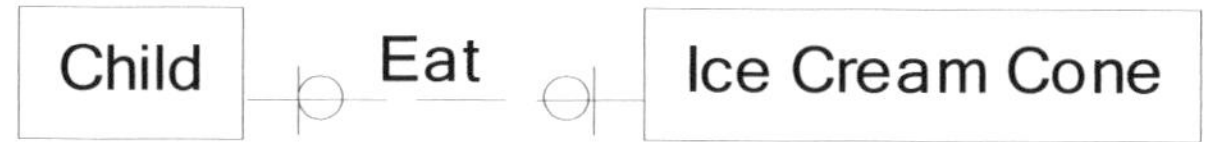

Example 2:

- Main topic not in center
- No verb phrases shown
- Supertype of Customer is not on top
- Relationship lines have many extra bends in them
- Relationship lines are too long—especially from Product to Customer and Product to Brand

Chapter 8
Now You Try It! Selecting the Correct Approach

Scenario	Approach taken	Explanation
Proposed data mart within a current data warehouse architecture. Available business users know exactly what they want.	Top-Down	Take full advantage of this rare opportunity. Most reporting applications are built from sketchy requirements, so consider yourself lucky to have more information.
Proposed new functionality to an existing operational or data mart application. IT resources are available but little involvement from the business.	Hybrid	Because we are dealing with an existing application and IT resources are available, it makes perfect sense to gather information from the existing system, and then meet with any business resources you can find (even if you have to camp out by the coffee machine), to discover and incorporate their requirements concepts.
Replacing an existing application. Both business and IT resources are available.	Hybrid	Information gathering should happen iteratively, starting with the existing application and then meeting with business resources to make enhancements.
Customization to packaged software. The business knows what they want and the packaged software documentation is poor. There are few technical resources who know the system.	Top-Down	We would start with the business requirements, but be careful: eventually you will need to understand at least a subset of the packaged software.

WORKS CITED

Adams, L. "Part I - Avalanche Judgment and Decision Making." Avalanche News, Selkirk College and the Selkirk Geospatial Research Center, Castlegar, BC, Vol. 74, Fall, 2005.

"The Data Warehousing Institute FlashPoint: Excerpt from the upcoming TDWI research report---The Rise of Analytic Applications: Build or Buy?" Data Warehousing Institute Sept. 25, 2002.

Hoberman, Steve. "Leveraging the Industry Logical Data Model as your Enterprise Data Model." 2006. Teradata. <www.teradata.com>.

Hoberman, Steve. "What's a Good Name for the High-Level Model?" DMReview. 1 Dec. 2008. http://www.dmreview.com/issues/2007_54/10002170-1.html

Mosley, M. DAMA Dictionary of Data Management. Technics Publications, LLC, 2008.

SUGGESTED READING

Burbank, Donna. "Get Some Respect in Data Management" Register Developer February (2008). <http://www.theregister.co.uk/2008/02/19/respect_data_management>.

Hay, D. Data Model Patterns: Conventions of Thought. Dorset House, 2000.

Hoberman, S. The Data Modeler's Workbench. John Wiley & Sons, Inc., 2001.

Hoberman, S. Data Modeling Made Simple. Technics Publications, LLC, 2005.

Maydanchik, A. Data Quality Assessment. Technics Publications, LLC, 2007.

Mosley, M. DAMA Dictionary of Data Management. Technics Publications, LLC, 2008.

Potts, C. FruITion: Creating the Ultimate Corporate Strategy for Information Technology. Technics Publications, LLC, 2008

Silverston, L. The Data Model Resource Book, Revised Edition, Volume 1, A Library of Universal Data Models For All Enterprises. John Wiley & Sons, Inc., 2001.

Silverston, L. The Data Model Resource Book, Revised Edition, Volume 2, A Library of Universal Data Models For Industry Types. John Wiley & Sons, Inc., 2001.

Simsion, G., and G. Witt. Data Modeling Essentials. Third ed. Morgan Kaufmann, 2005.